THE ART HANDBOOK

THE ART HANDBOOK

A subject-by-subject guide
to paintings and drawings

**Eagle
Editions**

AN OCEANA BOOK

Published by Eagle Editions Ltd
11 Heathfield
Royston
Hertfordshire SG8 5BW

This edition printed 2007

ISBN 1-84573-107-7

QUMTAH2

This book is produced by
Quantum Publishing Ltd
6 Blundell Street
London N7 9BH

Manufactured in Singapore by
Universal Graphics Pte. Ltd
Printed in Singapore by
Star Standard

CONTENTS

LEISURE

AT HOME

CITIES

LANDSCAPES

BELIEF

CONFLICT

ANIMALS

THE ARTIST'S LIFE

INTRODUCTION

No book about art can ever claim to be comprehensive since an infinite number of objects we call 'works of art' have been created throughout human history, representing innumerable belief-systems, stories and events, and they have been produced by different tools, techniques and materials.

If you want to understand something of this infinite variety, to see works of art in a comparative way, and to learn something from the techniques and viewpoints of those (often anonymous) makers of paintings and sculptures, we need to assemble our material in some sensible way.

Most art books adopt a chronological approach and focus on the stylistic similarities between works of art, often ignoring the significance of subject matter altogether. In this book we adopt a different approach, linking pictures by subject, in order to compare and contrast different treatments of various general themes.

We start with human life in its wider aspect, the stages of life, birth, copulation, death, emotions and so on. Work, the subject of chapter two follows, then leisure, itself related to work in various ways. Chapter four looks at the home as a place of work and domesticity, where in places like Japan, India and Holland it became the subject of a distinct genre in art. Then we pass from private to public space, from the home to the countryside and the city. Since representation of landscape as a distinct subject in painting emerged only from urbanized societies, it is logical to treat that next. The mystical and symbolic appreciation of nature is one aspect of a form of belief – a theme which in the broadest sense underlies the whole of this book. We look at belief in its specifically religious aspect in chapter seven – cults, mysteries, the religions of ancient Egypt, Greece, Rome, Christianity as illustrated by scenes from the Jewish Old Testament and the New Testament, Hinduism, Buddhism and Islam. Since belief often provoked prejudice and conflict, the chapter on war follows. Animals, the theme of chapter nine, often have specific mystical and symbolic associations; they also help us chart changing patterns of living, work, recreation and warfare. Finally, in chapter ten, we look at the world of the European painter, at the training of artists, the role of the market and at patterns of patronage and the tradition of the self-portrait.

The book can be used and read in any way – chapter ten, in fact, might well be read first. By selecting pictures thematically, however, we are forced to recognize that certain pictures are almost impossible to classify. For example, El Greco's *Christ Driving the Traders from the Temple* should be seen in the context of such diverse images as medieval condemnations of usury, as one of many variations on a theme from the life of Christ, as an attempt to visualize the long-destroyed Temple of Jerusalem, or as an anthology of figurative quotations from Michelangelo and painterly quotations from Titian and Tintoretto.

To understand these links we need to remember that artists have always been copyists and have always used other artists' works for their own ends. Before the invention of woodcuts, engraving, lithography and colour printing, young painters were often compelled to copy the works they admired, if only to learn from them and keep them as records for further use. In Europe, China and Japan, copying works by the masters was part of the training of every artist. Michelangelo studied Masaccio, Raphael quoted from the Sistine Chapel ceiling in *The School of Athens* (to Michelangelo's fury); Jan Steen quoted *The School of Athens* in his satirical *A School for Boys and Girls*. Such connections pervade this book and we cannot begin to spell them out in a few thousand words, but a reference bibliography is given at the end, so such threads can more easily be unravelled by the interested reader.

Copying and making variations on popular works was often a lucrative activity itself. When Pieter Bruegel the Elder died, his pictures were so scarce and in such demand that his sons and grandsons continued producing copies and variations on them for years. Sometimes the copy or variation is the only record we have of a lost masterpiece, like Cesare da Sesto's version of Leonardo's *Leda and the Swan*. Sometimes copies were commissioned, at other times they were deftly forged and sold as originals. Copies and forgeries proliferated to such an extent that many are still being sifted out – most major museums and galleries have basements full of them.

Collectors like that Archduke Leopold-Wilhelm commissioned Teniers to depict his gallery crammed with Titians, Correggios and Bassanois, and then he ordered him to make replicates of the paintings so that he could send them to impress his envious fellow princes.

Copying, as part of the training of the artist, survived later into the nineteenth century in Europe and its importance to artists like Manet, Gauguin and van Gogh is echoed in their many paintings which are variants on the old masters they had studied. Giorgione's lost Dresden *Venus* had inspired Titian's *Venus* or *Urbino*, Goya knew both when he painted his *Naked Maja*. Those pictures, and Ingres' *Grande Odalisque* in the Louvre, were all echoed in Manet's "modern" *Olympia* – the naked courtesan facing her visitor with a black cat at her feet (symbol of lust and Egyptian wisdom).

Towards the end of the nineteenth century, French artists also learned an immense amount from studying and copying woodcuts by Japanese masters like Hokusai and Hiroshige, prints which sold for less than a penny in the streets of Japan. The works of van Gogh, Gauguin and Toulouse-Lautrec display evidence of such influence.

Finally, it is worth emphasizing that works of art are crucial historical documents if we learn to read them carefully. In some instances, such as pre-Colombian art, they are the only surviving source of information, about a whole civilization. Obviously, though, a work like *The School of Athens*, which purports to represent the Platonic Academy in fifth-century BC Greece, is not a reliable source about Greece, but, interpreted cautiously, can tell us an immense amount about Humanist attitudes in early sixteenth-century Rome. Works that are clearly interpretative, even if non-figurative, can still tell us a lot about the attitudes and belief-systems of the artists who created them.

HUMAN LIFE

The theme of life is so wide-ranging that almost all art, in some sense, might be said to explore it. Work, leisure, the home, the city are all aspects of life; belief is essentially a metaphysical and systematic search for "the meaning of life"; war is an expression of the violence and life-denying forces in nature, and so on. Even a landscape in which no people are present might be seen as an expression of melancholy, solitude or withdrawal from the world, and animals, as we shall see, were often symbols of human virtues and vices. On the other hand, certain painters, like novelists and playwrights, have concentrated on the specifically human aspects of the world, and in their portrayal of common themes like maternity, birth, childhood, sex, senility, wisdom, madness and death, they have invested the subject with an emotional and psychological intensity which stresses the universality of the theme itself.

The books of the Bible, which underlay almost all European art for over a thousand years, provided innumerable themes for such treatment; the creation of Adam and Eve, the fall and expulsion from Paradise, the lives and suffering of the Old Testament prophets and the Israelites, and the themes of redemption symbolized by the birth and death of Christ, when treated by artists like Michelangelo, Grünewald, Bosch and Bruegel are more than merely religious narratives and they can easily be appreciated even if the story to which they relate is unknown.

During the Renaissance, artists increasingly began to use themes from classical Roman and Greek mythology, thus extending both subject matter and the expressive range of painting. It had hardly been possible to depict erotic desire and love within a Christian perspective, so that representations of the myths of Mars (war) overcome by Venus (love) Leda seduced by Jupiter disguised as a swan, and so on, provided the opportunity for an overly erotic and sensual manner of painting.

In northern Europe after the Reformation, artists began increasingly to dispense with such texts altogether; the Holy Family became a human family, Venus became Olympia, a courtesan, Adam became merely another male nude and the Old Testament story of Susanna bathing became an excuse for voyeurism on the part of the painter and the patron. Lust (one of the seven deadly sins) was often treated in such a way that the underlying moral was lost. Since lust, sex, ecstasy, eroticism, love, and marriage can all be confused and distinguished, sexual subjects have always fascinated artists and appealed to patrons, though only in India and Japan did a tradition of sexual art emerge unhindered by the criticism of moralists.

Death, no longer necessarily mediated by the Church, might be expressed in terms of landscape by artists like Friedrich, or dramatized as a scene of turbulent frenzy as in Delacroix's *The Death of Sardanapalus.* At the same time artists like Géricault and Goya managed to evoke the terrors of the imagination and the world of the insane with great insight and sympathy. From madness to the world of the outside is a short step, but, once again, artists like Rembrandt, Bosch and Géricault succeeded in capturing the dignity and suffering of society's outcasts.

Emotions are inevitably difficult to define and to distinguish one from another. Christian artists therefore either personified them (for example, Mary Magdalene symbolized grief and repentance) or portrayed them as pairs – love and envy, violence and remorse, excess and penitence. Allegories linking such themes were

Rembrandt, *Jacob Blessing the Children of Joseph*, (detail) 1656, oil on canvas, Gemäldegalerie, Kassel

particularly common in Italian and northern European art. In the nineteenth century the Realist tradition in France increasingly undermined the expressive potential of art, and it is only toward the end of the century that human emotion becomes once again the actual subject of painting, buttressed either by Symbolist ideas (in the case of artists like Moreau, Gauguin and Redon), which stressed the importance of the imagination, or in the twentieth century, in the work of artists like Dali (influenced by Freud) and Pollock (influenced by Jung).

The theme of class and status pervades all art. Here we concentrate on showing particular examples in terms of costume, pose and setting to bring out similarities and differences which are themselves socially determined.

LIFE

1 Edvard Munch, *The Dance of Life*, 1899, oil on canvas. Nasjonalgalleriet, Oslo

2 Casper David Friedrich, *The Stages of Life*, c 1835, oil on canvas. Museum der Bildenden Kunst, Leipzig

1

2

BIRTH

1 Joan Miro, *Maternity*, 1924, oil on canvas. Sir Roland Penrose Collection, London

2 Georges de La Tour, *The New Born*, c 1650, oil on canvas. Musée de Rennes

MOTHERHOOD

1 Edward Burne-Jones, *Earth Mother*, 1882, oil on canvas. Private Collection

2 Egon Schiele, *Mother with Two Children*, 1917, oil on canvas. Österreichisches Museum, Vienna

3 Pablo Picasso, *Woman and Child on a Beach*, c 1901, oil on canvas. Private Collection

4 Michelangelo, *Taddei Tondo*, c 1505, marble. Royal Academy of Arts, London

1

2

3

4

1

2

3

THE FAMILY

1 Paul Gauguin, *The Painter's Family in the Garden*, 1880, oil on canvas. Ny Carlsberg Glyptotek, Copenhagen

2 Goya, *Charles IV and his Family*, 1799–1800, oil on canvas. Prado, Madrid

3 The Brothers Le Nain, *The Family Meal*, c 1640, oil on canvas. Musée des Beaux Arts, Lille

4 Edgar Degas, *The Bellelli Family*, 1859–60, oil on canvas. Musée d'Orsay, Paris

4

CHILDHOOD

1 William Hogarth, *The Graham Children*, 1742, oil on canvas. Tate Gallery, London

2 Paula Modersohn-Becker, *Head of a Girl*, 1907, oil on canvas. Städelsches Kunstinstitut, Frankfurt

3 Anonymous American Artist, *The Hobby Horse*, c 1840, oil on panel. National Gallery of Art, Washington DC

4 Rembrandt, *Young Boy*, c 1660, oil on canvas. Norton Simon Foundation, Pasadena

1

2

3

4

1

YOUTH

1 Jan Toorop, *Les Trois Fiancées*, c 1892, ink and watercolour. Kroller-Muller Museum, Otterlo

2 Cosimo Rosselli, *Portrait of a Young Man*, c 1480, tempera on panel. Private Collection

3 Anonymous Benin Artist, *Queen Mother*, 16c, bronze. Museum für Völkerkunde, Berlin

2

3

LOVE

1 Antonio Canova, *Cupid and Psyche*, 1787–93, marble. Louvre, Paris

2 Anonymous French Artist, *Emblems of Love*, c 1500, watercolour. British Library, London

3 Gustav Klimt, *The Kiss*, 1907–8, oil on canvas. Kunsthistorisches Museum, Vienna

1

2

3

4

5

4 Workshop of Apollinio di Giovanni, *The Triumph of Love*, c 1460, tempera on panel. Victoria and Albert Museum, London

5 Gianlorenzo Bernini, *Ecstasy of St Teresa*, 1645–52, marble and bronze. Sta Maria della Vittoria, Rome

6 Anonymous Kangra Artist, *The Neglected Lady*, c 1850, watercolour. Victoria and Albert Museum, London

6

MARRIAGE

1 William Hogarth, *The Marriage*, plate 5 of *The Rake's Progress*, c 1734, oil on canvas. Sir John Soane's Museum, London

2 Rembrandt, *The Jewish Bride*, 1668, oil on canvas. Rijksmuseum, Amsterdam

3 Henri Rousseau, *La Noce (The Marriage)*, c 1910, oil on canvas. Musée d'Orsay, Paris

1

2

3

4

4 Jan van Eyck, *Arnolfini and his Bride*, 1434, oil on panel. National Gallery, London

THE NUDE

1 Jan van Eyck, *Eve*, from the right wing of the Ghent Altarpiece, 1425–8, oil on panel. St Bavo, Ghent

2 Albrecht Dürer, *Adam*, 1507, oil on panel. Prado, Madrid

3 Lucas Cranach, *Venus*, 1532, oil on canvas. Städelsches Kunstinstitut, Frankfurt

4 Michelangelo, *The Creation of Adam*, 1510, fresco. Sistine Chapel, Vatican, Rome

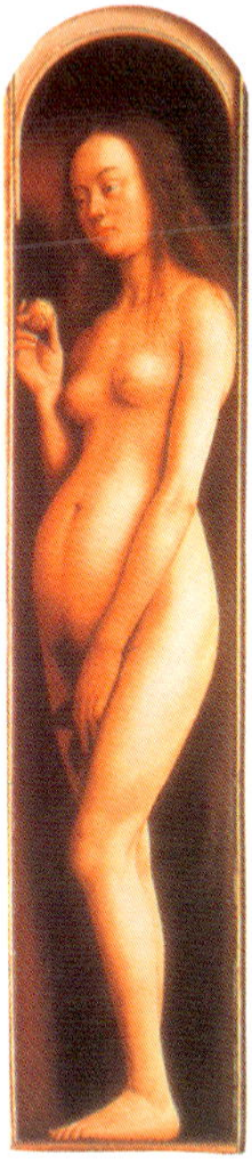

1

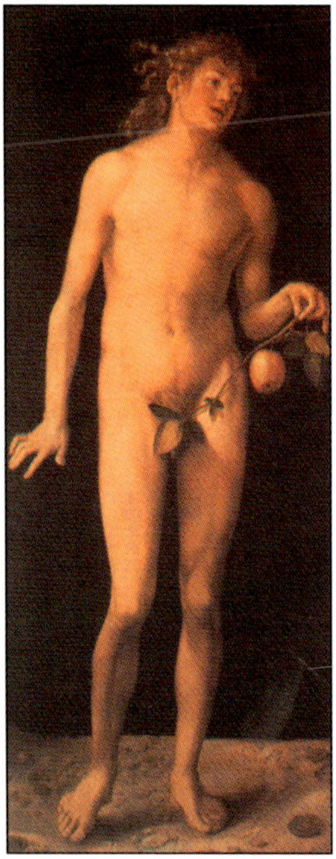

2

3

4

5 François Boucher, *Diana Getting out of her Bath*, 1742, oil on canvas. Louvre, Paris

6 Jacopo Tintoretto, *Susanna Bathing*, c 1560, oil on canvas. Kunsthistorishes Museum, Vienna

5

6

7 Edvard Munch, *Madonna*, c 1895, oil on canvas. Nasjonalgalleriet, Oslo

8 William Blake, *Satan and the Rebel Angels*, 1808, watercolour. Victoria and Albert Museum, London

9 Cesare da Sesto (after Leonardo da Vinci), *Leda and the Swan*, c 1510, oil on canvas. Wilton House, Wiltshire

7

8

9

10

11

10 Maesto Giorio, *The Three Graces*, 1525, glazed majolica roundel. Victoria and Albert Museum, London

11 Paul Gauguin, *Nevermore*, 1897, oil on canvas. Courtauld Institute Galleries, London

12 Amedeo Modigliani, *Seated Nude*, c 1917, oil on canvas. Private Collection

13 Jean-Auguste Ingres, *La Grande Odalisque*, 1814, oil on canvas. Louvre, Paris

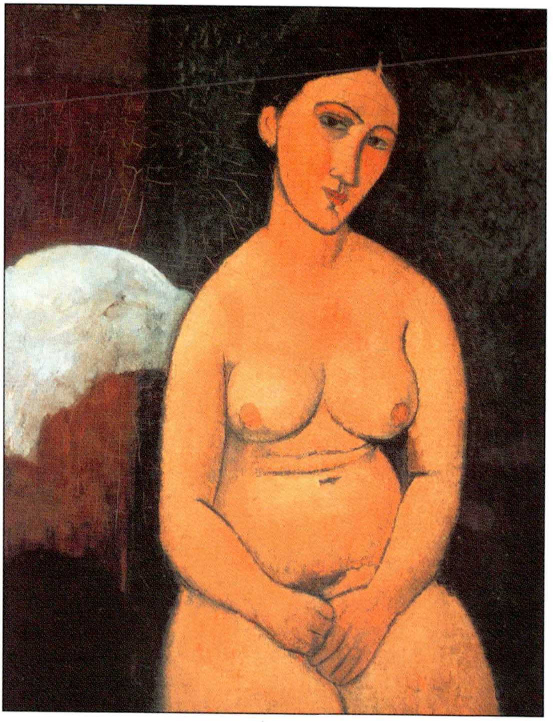

12

13

14

15

16

17

14 Edouard Manet, *Olympia*, 1863, oil on canvas. Louvre, Paris

15 Gustave Courbet, *The Bathers* (detail), 1853, oil on canvas. Musée Fabre, Montpellier

16 Jean-Auguste Ingres, *Jupiter and Thetis*, 1811, oil on canvas. Musée Granet, Aix-en-Provence

17 Goya, *The Naked Maja*, 1797–1800, oil on canvas. Prado, Madrid

18 Edgar Degas, *The Young Spartans*, begun 1860, oil on canvas. National Gallery, London

19 Jean-Auguste Ingres, *Oedipus and the Sphinx*, 1808/27, oil on canvas. Louvre, Paris

20 John Heinrich Fuseli, *The Creation of Eve*, c 1770, oil on canvas. Private Collection

21 Théodore Géricault, *Half-length Portrait of a Nude Man*, c 1816, oil on canvas. Private Collection

18

19

20

21

OLD AGE

1

2

3

4

5

1 Luca Giordano, *The Good Samaritan* (detail), late 17c, oil on canvas. Musée des Beaux Arts, Rouen

2 After Quentin Massys, *Grotesque Old Woman*, c 1520, oil on wood. National Gallery, London

3 Rembrandt, *Old Woman Reading*, 1655, oil on canvas. Drumlanrig Castle, Scotland

4 Filippino Lippi, *Portrait of an Old Man*, 1485, fresco on tile. Uffizi, Florence

5 Gustave Courbet, *Old Man with a Glass of Wine*, c 1860, oil on canvas. Mayor Gallery, London

DEATH

1 Pieter Bruegel the Elder, *The Triumph of Death*, c 1562, oil on panel. Prado, Madrid

1

2 Anonymous Flemish Artist, *Young Woman on her Deathbed*, 17c, oil on canvas. Musée des Beaux Arts, Rouen

3 Paul Cézanne, *A Murder*, 1867–70, oil on canvas. Walker Art Gallery, Liverpool

4 Nicolas Poussin, *The Massacre of the Innocents*, 1630s, oil on canvas. Musée Condé, Chantilly

2

3

4

5

6

5 J.M.W. Turner, *Burial at Sea*, 1842, oil on canvas. Tate Gallery, London

6 Eugène Delacroix, *The Death of Sardanapalus*, 1844, oil on canvas. Louvre, Paris

7 Andrea Mantegna, *The Dead Christ*, c 1480, tempera on canvas. Brera, Milan

8 Anonymous Egyptian Artist, *Shepermut, Priestess of Thebes*, c 800 BC, tempera on wood. Royal Albert Memorial Museum, Exeter

9 Odilon Redon, *The Angel of Destiny*, c 1890, oil on canvas. Private Collection

7

8

9

10

11

12

10 Samael, *The Angel of Destiny*, c 1500, watercolour. National Library, Vienna

11 Giotto, *The Death of St Francis*, c 1360, fresco. Sta Croce, Florence

12 Carlos Schwabe, *The Angel of Death*, 1900, oil on canvas. Musée d'Orsay, Paris

SEX AND LUST

1 Peter Paul Rubens, *Nereid and Triton*, 1630, oil on canvas. Boymans-van Beuningen Museum, Rotterdam

2 Anonymous Ganges Valley Artist, *Courtesan and her Client*, 19c, watercolour. Victor Lowndes Collection, London

3 Kitagawa Utamaro, *Lovers*, from *The Poem of the Pillow*, 1788, woodblock print. Victoria and Albert Museum, London

4 Katsushika Hokusai, *Awabi Fisherwoman and Octopus*, 1820–30, woodblock print. British Museum, London

1

2

3

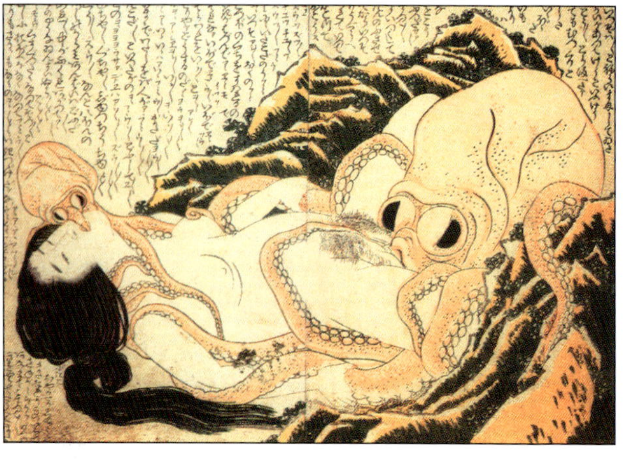

4

5

5 Max Ernst, *Men Shall Know Nothing of This*, 1923, oil on canvas. Tate Gallery, London

6 Auguste Rodin, *The Kiss*, c 1890, marble. Musée Rodin, Paris

7 Gustave Courbet, *Le Sommeil (Sleep)*, 1866, oil on canvas. Musée du Petit Palais, Paris

6

7

8

8 Hieronymus Bosch, *The Garden of Earthly Delights* (detail), c 1500, oil on panel. Prado, Madrid

9

9 William Hogarth, *The Orgy*, plate 3 from *A Rake's Progress*, 1734, oil on canvas. Sir John Soane's Museum, London

THE EMOTIONS

1 Pablo Picasso, *Weeping Woman*, 1937, oil on canvas. Sir Roland Penrose Collection, London

2 William Blake, *Pity*, c 1795, watercolour. Tate Gallery, London

1

2

3

4

5

6

3 Albrecht Dürer, *Melencolia*, 1514, woodcut. Private Collection

4 Rogier van der Weyden, *Mary Magdalene Weeping*, 1450–2, oil on panel. Louvre, Paris

5 Paul Sérusier, *Melancholia* or *Breton Eve*, c 1890, oil on canvas. Musée d'Orsay, Paris

6 William Blake, *The Body of Abel Found by Adam and Eve*, c 1824, watercolour on wood. Tate Gallery, London

7 Jackson Pollock, *The Moon – Woman Cuts the Circle*, c 1943, oil on canvas. Musée d'Art Moderne, Paris

8 George Hicks, *Alone*, 1878, oil on canvas. Christopher Wood Gallery, London

9 Georges de La Tour, *Mary Magdalene with a Night Lamp*, 1630–35, oil on canvas. Louvre, Paris

7

8

9

10

11

10 Caspar David Friedrich, *The Wanderer*, c 1815, oil on canvas. Kunsthalle, Hamburg

11 Théodore Géricault, *The Raft of the Medusa* (sketch), 1817, oil on canvas. Louvre, Paris

12 Edvard Munch, *The Scream*, 1893, oil on canvas. Nasjonalgalleriet, Oslo

12

13 Pieter Bruegel the Younger, *French Proverbs*, c 1610, oil on canvas. Private Collection

14 Agnolo Bronzino, *An Allegory of Cupid, Love, Envy, Deceit and Time*, c 1550, oil on canvas. National Gallery, London

15 Lucas Cranach, *The Effects of Jealousy*, 1535, oil on panel. Louvre, Paris

13

14

15

16

16 Holman Hunt, *The Awakening Conscience*, 1853, oil on canvas. Tate Gallery, London

17 Giovanni Bellini, *An Allegory of Prudence and Vanity*, c 1490, oil on panel. Accademia, Venice

18 Simon Vouet, *Lucretia and Tarquin*, c 1620, oil on canvas. Private Collection

17

18

CHARITY

1

1 Cornelis Buys, *Feeding the Hungry*, 1504, oil on panel. Rijksmuseum, Amsterdam

2

3

4

5

2 David Vinckboons, *The Blind Hurdy-Gurdy Player*, c 1620, oil on panel. Johnny van Haeften Gallery, London

3 Theodore van Baburen, *Cimon and Pero: Roman Charity*, c 1625, oil on canvas. City Art Gallery, York

4 Pieter Bruegel the Younger, *The Seven Acts of Mercy*, c 1600, oil on canvas. Private Collection

5 Pieter Bruegel the Elder, *The Cripples*, 1568, oil on panel. Louvre, Paris

DRUNKENNESS

1 Anonymous Flemish Artist, *Allegory of Temperance and Excess* (detail), 1540–60, oil on canvas. Private Collection

2 Jan Steen, *The Effects of Intemperance*, 1662–3, oil on canvas. National Gallery, London

3 Edgar Degas, *L'Absinthe*, 1876, oil on canvas. Louvre, Paris

4 Pieter de Hooch, *Woman Drinking with Soldiers*, 1658, oil on canvas. Louvre, Paris

1

2

3

4

THE FIVE SENSES

1

2

3

4

1 Philippe Mercier, *The Five Senses – Taste*, c 1720, oil on canvas. Roy Miles Fine Paintings, London

2 Philippe Mercier, *The Five Senses – Hearing*, c 1720, oil on canvas. Roy Miles Fine Paintings, London

3 Nicholas Hilliard, *Young Man among Flowers*, c 1587, watercolour on wood. Victoria and Albert Museum, London

4 Abraham Govaerts, *The Five Senses*, c 1600, oil on canvas. Louvre, Paris

WISDOM

1 Andrea Mantegna, *The Triumph of Wisdom over Evil*, 1505, tempera on canvas. Louvre, Paris

2 Michelangelo, *The Libyan Sibyl*, 1511, fresco. Sistine Chapel, Vatican, Rome

3 Auguste Rodin, *The Thinker*, 1880, bronze. Musée Rodin, Paris

1

2

3

1

MADNESS

1 William Hogarth, *The Madhouse*, plate 7 from *A Rake's Progress*, 1735, oil on canvas. Sir John Soane's Museum, London

2 Théodore Géricault, *Portrait of an Insane Woman*, c 1822, oil on canvas. Louvre, Paris

3 Théodore Géricault, *Portrait of an Insane Man*, c 1822, oil on canvas. Museum of Fine Art, Springfield, Mass

2

3

DREAMS

1 Salvador Dali, *The Persistence of Memory*, 1931, oil on canvas. Museum of Modern Art, New York

2 Matthias Grünewald, *The Temptation of St Anthony* from The Isenheim Altarpiece, c 1515, oil on panel. Unterlinden Museum, Colmar

3 Goya, *The Bewitched Man*, c 1798, oil on canvas. National Gallery, London

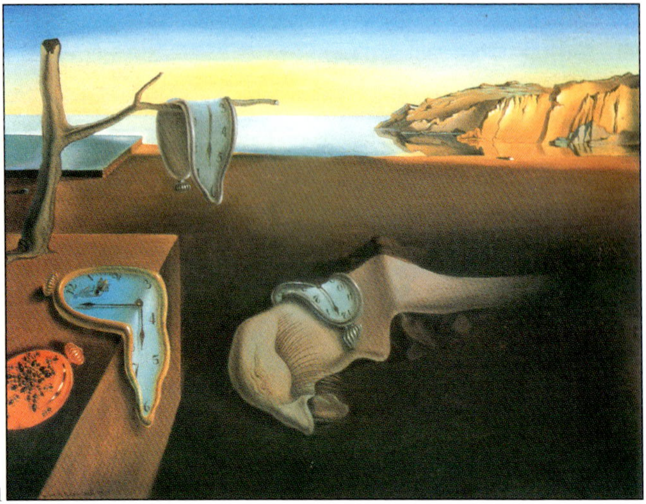

1

2

3

OUTSIDERS

1

2

3

4

5

1 Hieronymus Bosch, *The Vagabond (The Prodigal Son?)*, c 1500, oil on panel. Boymans-van Beuningen Museum, Rotterdam

2 Rembrandt, *An Oriental*, 1635, oil on panel. Chatsworth House, Derbyshire

3 David Teniers the Younger, *The Gypsies*, c 1670, oil on canvas. Musée des Beaux Arts, Lille

4 Théodore Géricault, *Head of a Negro*, c 1817, oil on canvas. Private Collection

5 Antoine Watteau, *Head of a Negro*, c 1715, chalk on paper. British Museum, London

CLASS & STATUS

1 Marcus Gheeraerts, *Queen Elizabeth I*, c 1592, oil on panel. Woburn Abbey, Bedfordshire

2 Jean-Auguste Ingres, *Mlle Rivière*, 1805, oil on canvas. Louvre, Paris

3 Francesco Bacchiacca, *Portrait of a Lady*, c 1530, oil on panel. Private Collection

1

2

3

4

4 Claude Monet, *Women in the Garden*, 1866–7, oil on canvas. Musée d'Orsay, Paris

5

5 Rembrandt, *The Syndicates*, 1661, oil on canvas. Rijksmuseum, Amsterdam

WORK

When pictures like Courbet's *The Stonebreakers* and Millet's *The Sower* were first exhibited, they provoked torrents of criticism and abuse, so offended was the bourgeois public by depictions of labour as heroic and threatening. Yet since Egyptian times men and women at work had been a common theme in painting. Medieval illuminated manuscripts in particular equated the changing patterns of work with the seasons, and medieval calenders, like that of the Limburg brothers, provide a remarkably detailed account of rural labour in pre-modern societies – sowing, weeding, harvesting, tending cattle, killing pigs for the winter and so on. These were all familiar subjects which Bruegel, in his great cycle of paintings (some now lost, the rest in Vienna), translated into full scale canvases in which he created perhaps the most potent image of the agricultural year yet devised.

Craftsmen at work are also common subjects in Indian as well as Christian art, which often laid particular emphasis on the occupations of the saints like fishing and carpentry. Sometimes subjects like the marriage feast at Cana and the last supper were set in the background to allow the depiction of commonplace domestic tasks like cooking. Many of these scenes also conveyed moral messages as in the pictures of banking and bankers which were representations of the sin of usury, or Bosch's *Cure of Folly*, which is a comment on both the tricks of quack doctors and the gullibility of their victims. The theme of construction work is also common in European art with scenes like the building of *The Tower of Babel* and *The Construction of the Temple of Jerusalem* providing detailed information about various craft practices of the time.

On the other hand, the increasing secularization of society and the growing importance of portraiture meant that even merchants and lawyers could be painted without moralizing. Holbein's portrait of *George Grisze*, for example, stresses the sitter's gentility and intellectual status, far removed from the usual grubby associations of commerce.

Flemish artists seem to have been the first to treat work as a genre in its own right, and in the hands of later painters like Vermeer, Velazquez and Chardin, the commonplace subject is dignified by the artistry of the painter. Chardin's reputation was in fact so great that, almost single-handed, he forced the public to accept domestic labour as a worthy subject for art. Thus subsequent artists like Manet, Degas and Pissarro, when dealing with such themes, were working in a well-established tradition.

The rapid transformation of the English landscape in the eighteenth century and the introduction of industrial processes were well documented in England by artists like de Loutherbourg, Joseph Wright and Turner, and paintings of factory scenes and the new industrial processes help us document the revolution in the nature of work in industrial societies.

Increasing class divisions are also reflected in painting, with certain professions like medicine, the law and teaching often portrayed. The achievements of Greek philosophy were evoked by Raphael in an heroic representation of the great philosophers and mathematicians of the ancient world, while Wright's masterpiece, *An Experiment with the Airpump*, conjures up not the world of the past, but the achievements of the present in his group portrait of Joseph Priestley the chemist, Wedgwood the industrialist and Erasmus Darwin. Similarly a much more honest depiction of the world of prostitution, of the courtesan and the brothel – although often romanticized by lesser artists like Gervex in *Rolla* – is shown by Manet and Toulouse-Lautrec.

Anonymous Flemish Artist, *December: Pig Killing, tug of war with sledges*, early 16c calendar, watercolour. British Library, London

AGRICULTURE

1 Anonymous Roman Artist, *Spring* or *Flora*, 1c AD, fresco. Archaeological Museum, Naples

1

2

3

2 Jean-François Millet, *The Sower*, 1850, oil on canvas. Museum of Fine Arts, Boston

3 Anonymous, *The Sower*, 14c, stained glass. Canterbury Cathedral

4 Pol de Limburg, *Les Très Riches Heures du Duc de Berry, March*, c 1415, Musée Condé, Chantilly

5 Andrea Riccio, *Boy Milking a Goat*, c 1510, bronze. Private Collection

6 Sebastian Vrancx, *Summer*, c 1620, oil on canvas. Roy Miles Fine Paintings, London

7 Pol de Limburg, *Les Très Riches Heures – July*, c 1415, Musée Condé, Chantilly

8 Anonymous Egyptian Artist, *Harvest Scenes*, 19th Dynasty (c 1320–1100 BC), tempera on plaster. Valley of the Nobles, Thebes

6

7

8

9

9 Pieter Bruegel the Elder, *Haymakers – June* (detail), 1565, oil on panel. Narodni Museum, Prague

10 Pol de Limburg, *Les Très Riches Heures – September*, c 1415, Musée Condé, Chantilly

11 Anonymous French Artist, *Picking Apples*, late 15c, watercolour. British Library, London

12 Camille Pissarro, *The Haymaker*, 1884, oil on canvas. Private Collection

10

11

12

13

14

15

13 George Stubbs, *Labourers*, 1785, enamel on biscuit and earthenware. Tate Gallery, London

14 Jean-François Millet, *The Gleaners*, 1857, oil on canvas. Louvre, Paris

15 Samuel Palmer, *The Cornfield*, c 1830, watercolour. Tate Gallery, London

16 Inigerebig Penestan, *Harvest Scene – Bali*, c 1960, watercolour. Private Collection

17 Paul Gauguin, *The Seaweed Gatherers*, 1889, oil on canvas. Folkwang Museum, Essen

16

17

18

19

18 Linton Park, *Flax Scutching Bee Party*, c 1860, oil on panel. National Gallery of Art, Washington DC

19 Anonymous Egyptian Artist, *Fowling*, c 1410 BC, tempera on plaster. Valley of the Nobles, Thebes

20 Pieter Bruegel the Elder, *Hunters in the Snow – February,* 1565, oil on panel. Kunsthistorisches Museum, Vienna

21 Pieter Bruegel the Elder, *Return of the Herd – December,* 1565, oil on panel. Kunsthistorisches Museum, Vienna

20

21

22 Thomas Poynitz, *November/December*, late 17c, Mortlake tapestry. Victoria and Albert Museum, London

22

FISHING

1 Theo van Rysselberghe, *The Man on the Tiller*, 1892, oil on canvas. Musée d'Orsay, Paris

2 Katsushika Hokusai, *Fisherman in Kai Province*, c 1830, woodblock print. Private Collection

1

2

3 J.M.W. Turner, *Fishermen on a Lee Shore*, c 1805, oil on canvas. Iveagh Bequest, Kenwood House, London

4 Il Domenichino, *Fishermen on an Estuary*, c 1610, oil on canvas. Private Collection

5 Konrad Witz, *Miraculous Draught of Fishes*, 1444, oil on panel. Musée d'Art et d'Histoire, Geneva

3

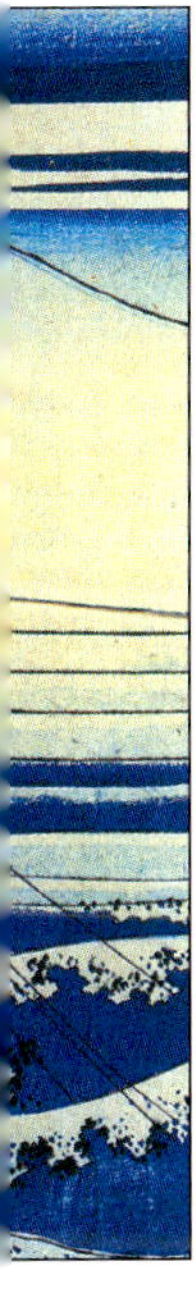

4

5

CRAFTS

1 Anonymous Flemish Artist, *Vulcan's Forge*, 16c, oil on panel. Musée des Beaux Arts, Lille

2 Joseph Wright, *The Iron Forge*, 1772, oil on canvas. Private Collection

1

2

3 J.M.W. Turner, *A Blacksmith's Shop*, c 1807, black and brown wash. British Museum, London

4 Anonymous Egyptian Artist, *Engraving and Polishing Vases in Gold and Silver*, 18th Dynasty, tempera on plaster. Valley of the Nobles, Thebes

3

4

5 Anonymous Egyptian Artist, *Carpenters Working with Adzes*, 18th Dynasty (c 1410 BC), tempera on plaster. Valley of the Nobles, Thebes

6 Gulam Ali Khan, *A Village Scene in the Punjab*, c 1820, watercolour. India Office Library, London

7 Bayeux Tapestry, *Building the Boats*, c 1080, embroidery. Musée de la Tapisserie de Bayeux

5

6

7

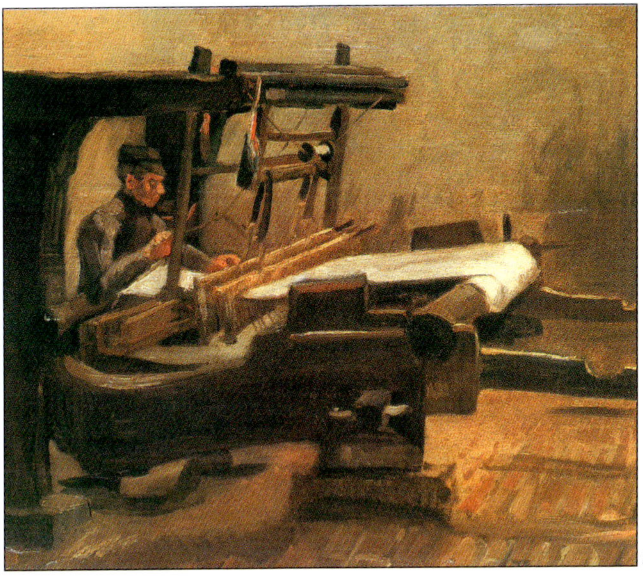

8

9

8 Vincent van Gogh, *The Weaver*, 1884, oil on canvas. Private Collection

9 Frank Holl, *The Song of the Shirt*, 1874, oil on canvas. Royal Albert Memorial Museum, Exeter

BUILDING

1 Edouard Manet, *Roadmenders in the Rue de Berne*, 1878, oil on canvas. National Gallery, London

2 Anonymous Artist, *The Building of Marseilles*, mid 15c, watercolour. British Library, London

3 Joseph and Jean Fouquet, *Construction of the Temple of Jerusalem under the Orders of King Solomon*, c 1475, watercolour. Bibliothèque Nationale, Paris

4 Miskina and Serwan, *The Red Fort at Agra during its Construction in 1562*, c 1590, watercolour. Victoria and Albert Museum, London

5 Abel Grimmer, *Parable of the Rich Man who Built Greater Barns*, late 16c, oil on canvas. Private Collection

1

2

3

4

5

6 Goya, *The Injured Mason*, 1787, oil on canvas. Prado, Madrid

6

7 Fernand Léger, *Les Constructeurs*, 1950, oil on canvas. Musée Léger, Biot

8 Edward Poynter, *Israel in Egypt*, 1867, oil on canvas. Guildhall Art Gallery, London

7

8

9

9 Anonymous French Artist, *Noah Building the Ark*, 1423, watercolour. British Library, London

10

10 Pieter Bruegel the Elder, *The Tower of Babel*, c 1560, oil on panel. Kunsthistorisches Museum, Vienna

11 Joseph Vernet, *Construction of a Road*, 1774, oil on canvas. Louvre, Paris

12 Jan van Grevebroeck, *Dredging a Canal*, c 1770, oil on canvas. Civico Museo Correr, Venice

13 Gustave Courbet, *The Stonebreakers*, 1849, oil on canvas. Formerly the Staatliche Gemäldegalerie, Dresden (destroyed)

11

12

13

14

15

14 Jean-François Millet, *The Wood Sawyers*, 1850–2, oil on canvas. Victoria and Albert Museum, London

15 Robert Campin?, *St Joseph* (portrayed as a medieval carpenter), from The Merode Altarpiece, c 1425, oil on panel. Metropolitan Museum of Art, New York

16

16 Gustave Caillebotte, *The Planers of the Parquet*, 1875, oil on canvas. Musée d'Orsay, Paris

G. Caillebotte
1875

INDUSTRY

1 Eyre Crowe, *Dinner Hour at Wigan*, 1874, oil on canvas. City Art Gallery, Manchester

2 Anonymous, *Filling Tea Chests, Canton*, c 1820, oil on canvas. Private Collection

1

2

3

4

5

3 Thomas Hare, *The Shaft Bottom*, c 1845, watercolour. Department of Mining, University of Newcastle-upon-Tyne

4 E.J. Delahaye, *The Gas Factory at Courcelles*, 1884, oil on canvas. Musée du Petit Palais, Paris

5 Fernand Cormon, *Interior of a Factory*, c 1870, oil on canvas. Musée d'Orsay, Paris

6 Jean-Charles Develly, *Gobelins Factory*, 1840, watercolour. Musée Carnavalet, Paris

7 Bart van der Leck, *Return from the Factory*, 1908, ink and poster paint. Rijksmuseum, Amsterdam

6

7

8

8 William James Muller, *Forging the Anchor*, 1831, oil on canvas. City Art Gallery, Bristol

9 *Associated Shipwrights' Society Emblem*, 1880, printed cotton. Trades Union Congress, London

10 William Bell Scott, *Industry on the Tyne – Iron and Coal*, c 1855, oil and tempera on plaster. National Trust, Wallington Hall, Northumberland

9

10

DOMESTIC WORK

1 Itō Shinsui, *Girl Washing Linen*, 1917, woodblock print, British Museum, London

1

2 Edgar Degas, *Woman Ironing*, c 1885, oil on canvas. Walker Art Gallery, Liverpool

3 Henri de Toulouse-Lautrec, *Woman Filling a Basin*, 1896, lithograph. Private Collection

2

3

4 D.E.J. de Noter, *A Maid in the Kitchen*, 1850s, oil on canvas. Private Collection

5 Jan Vermeer, *Lady with a Milk Jug*, c 1665, oil on canvas. Rijksmuseum, Amsterdam

6 Jan Vermeer, *The Lacemaker*, c 1760, oil on canvas. Louvre, Paris

7 Quiringh Gerritsz van Brekelenkam, *A Kitchen Interior*, 1660s, oil on panel. Johnny van Haeften Gallery, London

4

5

6

7

8

9

10

8 Jean-Honoré Fragonard, *Washerwomen in a Garden*, c 1770, oil on canvas. Musée de Picardie, Amiens

9 Camille Pissarro, *Woman Hanging out her Washing*, 1887, oil on canvas. Musée d'Orsay, Paris

10 Jean-Baptiste Chardin, *The Scullery Maid*, 1738, oil on canvas. Hunterian Art Gallery, Glasgow

11 Anonymous Flemish Artist, *The Supper at Emmaus*, 16c, oil on canvas. Musée des Beaux Arts, Lille

11

COMMODITIES

1 Marinus van Reymerswaele, *The Tax Collector*, c 1530, oil on panel. Musée des Beaux Arts, Valenciennes

2 Agustino Brunias, *A Linen Stall and a Vegetable Seller in the Caribbean*, c 1770, oil on canvas. Private Collection

1

2

3

3 Pieter Bruegel the Elder, *Tax Collecting*, 1556, oil on canvas. Prado, Madrid

4 Workshop of Lucas van Valkenborch, *Vegetable Market*, 1590, oil on canvas. Kunsthistorisches Museum, Vienna

5 Anonymous Italian Artist, *The Pharmacy Shop*, 15c fresco. Villa Issogna, Val d'Aosta

4

5

6 Edgar Degas, *Cotton Exchange in New Orleans*, 1873, oil on canvas. Musée d'Orsay, Paris

7 Robert Dighton, *Stockjobbers Extraordinary*, c 1795, ink and watercolour. Guildhall Library, London

8 Anonymous, *Italian Bankers – Usury*, 15c, manuscript. British Library, London

6

7

8

9 Velazquez, *The Water Seller of Seville*, c 1620, oil on canvas. Apsley House, London

10 Charles Pierron, *In the Bazaar*, c 1870, watercolour. Private Collection

9

10

TEACHING

1 Jean-Baptiste Chardin, *The Schoolmistress*, 1735–6, oil on canvas. National Gallery, London

2 Jan Steen, *A School for Boys and Girls*, 1663–5, oil on canvas. National Gallery of Scotland, Edinburgh

1

2

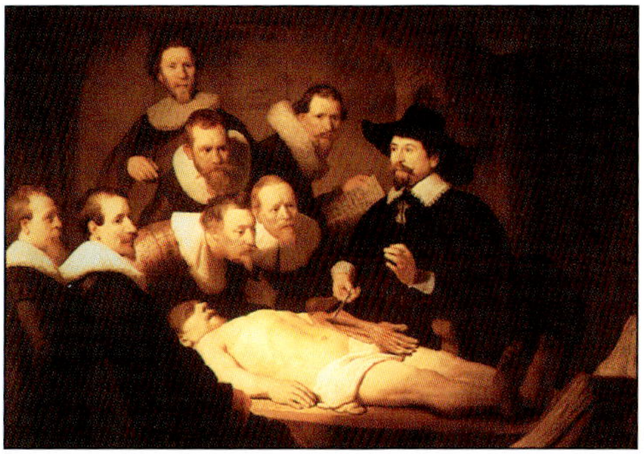

1

2

3

MEDICINE

1 Rembrandt, *The Anatomy Lesson*, 1632, oil on panel. Mauritshuis, The Hague

2 Hieronymus Bosch, *The Cure of Folly*, c 1550, oil on panel. Prado, Madrid

3 Rembrandt, *The Anatomy Lesson*, 1656, oil on canvas. Rijksmuseum, Amsterdam

THE PROFESSIONS

1 Raphael, *The School of Athens*, 1510–11, fresco. Vatican, Rome

2 Hans Holbein, *George Grisze*, 1532, oil on panel. Staatliche Gemäldegalerie, Berlin

1

2

3

4

5

6

3 Joseph Wright of Derby, *An Experiment with the Air Pump*, 1768, oil on canvas. Tate Gallery, London

4 Adrian van Ostade, *Lawyer in his Study*, 1637, oil on canvas. Boymans-van Beuningen Museum, Rotterdam

5 Edouard Manet, *Emile Zola in his Study*, 1867–8, oil on canvas. Musée d'Orsay, Paris

6 Quentyn Massys, *The Notary*, c 1515, oil on panel. Private Collection

PROSTITUTION

1 Henri de Toulouse-Lautrec, *The Salon in the Rue des Moulins,* 1894, oil on canvas. Musée Toulouse-Lautrec, Albi

2 Henri Gervex, *Rolla,* 1878, oil on canvas. Musée des Beaux Arts, Bordeaux

3 Edouard Manet, *Nana,* 1877, oil on canvas. Kunsthalle, Hamburg

1

2

3

4

4 Ernst Ludwig Kirchner, *Street Scene*, 1913, oil on canvas. Staatsgalerie, Stuttgart

LEISURE

Play and recreation are common to all societies, though the degree to which people can relax and enjoy their leisure varies enormously. Sex, class, cultural and age differences also influence the ways in which pleasures are chanelled and permitted in all societies, with the tacit acknowledgement that while the rich have both more time and money to indulge their tastes, the poor are expected to work, and only enjoy themselves in limited ways. The rituals of popular entertainment and the provision of the simplest of toys could nevertheless result in innumerable pleasures as Bruegel's great painting shows. Furthermore, one person's leisure is often dependent upon another's labour, as many of these circus, theatre, marriage and inn scenes make explicit.

Religious festivals throughout Christian Europe became the focus of communal recreation, as well as being occasions for markets, street entertainments, drinking and love-making. That some of those festivals hark back to the rituals and beliefs of pre-Christian cults is evident from paintings like Goya's *Burial of the Sardine* and Manet's *Bullfight.* Such festivals were invariably associated with feasting and drinking, and in Flemish and Dutch painting in particular, a moralizing message against drunkenness, lechery and gluttony was clearly intended. Gambling scenes also attracted Flemish and Dutch artists who liked to stress the avarice of crooked gamblers and gullibility of simple-minded punters, and satirists like Rowlandson in *The Hazard Room* saw gambling in eighteenth-century England as a metaphor for greed itself.

The linked pleasures of music and dancing are celebrated in almost every culture from that of ancient Egypt and the Orient to classical and modern Europe. Music also symbolized the sense of hearing and, unlike other pleasures, was not condemned by the Church – *King David playing his Harp* and Orpheus charming the animals were common musical themes in European art, while in Mughal India pictures were often intended to convey particular musical themes.

Naturally, leisure has a context. The different worlds of men and women in bourgeois Europe is particularly marked in painting where women are often depicted alone in their homes, reading, writing, dressing and decorating themselves or perhaps waiting for lovers. The subject of *fêtes champêtre* or picnics was popular, not simply because of the possibility it offered of linking a contemporary scene to the delights of landscape, though when Manet, in *Déjenuer sur l'herbe,* produced a modern version of Giorgione-Titian's painting, the explicit eroticism of the scene outraged contemporary morality.

Theatre scenes are common to both Japanese and European art, though the intention is often more than mere entertainment; Watteau's *Commedia dell'Arte,* for example, stresses both the melancholy and artifice of theatre, while painters like Degas and Manet concentrated as often on the spectators as on the stage.

Sport too has been a popular theme for artists since ancient times; wrestlers, boxers and charioteers decorate innumerable Greek vases, as do hunting scenes and bullfights. Hunting became a courtly pleasure both in medieval Europe and in Mughal India where particular animals were reserved for the dangerous and dubious pleasures of the nobility and where artists were commissioned to record the heroic and bloody exploits of their masters.

Goya, *The Love Letter*, 1811–14, oil on canvas. Musée des Beaux Arts, Lille

Bourgeois recreation on the other hand was a common theme for the early Impressionists, in part because of the importance they attached to contemporary subjects, whether it were scenes of boating, bathing, sitting in the sun or seduction. By contrast paintings like *L'Absinthe* by Degas, Gauguin's *Night Café*, Toulouse-Lautrec's bar and brothel scenes, or Modigliani's solitary drinker are pervaded by profound melancholy.

FESTIVALS

1 Claude Monet, *Rue St Denis, Fête,* 1878, oil on canvas. Musée des Beaux Arts, Rouen

2 Abel Grimmer, *A Cardinal on the Feast Day of St George in a Village near Antwerp,* c 1605, oil on canvas. Private Collection

1

2

3

3 Samuel Coleman, *St James' Fair*, 1824, oil on canvas. City Art Gallery, Bristol

4

4 Goya, *Burial of the Sardine*, 1791–2, oil on canvas. Prado, Madrid

GAMBLING

1 George Caleb Bingham, *Ferrymen Playing Cards*, 1847, oil on canvas. St Louis Art Museum, Missouri

2 Dirk Hals, *The Game of Backgammon*, c 1630, oil on canvas. Musée des Beaux Arts, Lille

3 Georges de La Tour, *The Cheat with the Ace of Diamonds*, c 1635, oil on canvas. Louvre, Paris

1

2

3

4

4 Thomas Rowlandson, *The Hazard Room*, 1792, watercolour. Victoria and Albert Museum, London

5

5 Anonymous English Artist, *Rat Catching at the Blue Anchor Tavern*, 1850–2, oil on canvas. Museum of London

DRINK

1 Edouard Manet, *At Père Lathuille's*, c 1879, oil on canvas. Musée des Beaux Arts, Tournai

2 Michelangelo da Caravaggio, *Young Bacchus*, c 1600, oil on canvas. Uffizi, Florence

3 Amedeo Modigliani, *A Seated Man Leaning on a Table*, c 1917, oil on canvas. Jesi Collection, Milan

1

2

3

4

5

6

4 Paul Gauguin, *Night Café, Arles*, 1881, oil on canvas. Museum of Western Art, Moscow

5 Henri de Toulouse-Lautrec, *In a Private Room at the Rat Mort*, 1899, oil on canvas. Courtauld Institute Galleries, London

6 Jan Steen, *Tavern Interior*, c 1660, oil on canvas. Johnny van Haeften Gallery, London

FEASTS

1 Adriaen van Ostade, *Barn Interior with Boors Carousing at a Wedding*, c 1650, oil on canvas. Private Collection

2 Pierre-Auguste Renoir, *Luncheon of the Boating Party, Bougival*, 1881, oil on canvas. Phillips Collection, Washington DC

1

2

3

3 Pieter Bruegel the Elder, *The Peasants' Wedding*, c 1568, oil on panel. Kunsthistorisches Musuem, Vienna

4 Anonymous, *John of Portugal entertains John of Gaunt*, late 15c, watercolour. British Library, London

4

MUSIC

1 Pierre-Auguste Renoir, *Young Girls at a Piano*, 1892, oil on canvas. Private Collection

2 Edgar Degas, *The Musicians of the Orchestra*, 1868–70, oil on canvas. Louvre, Paris

3 Anonymous, *Roman Artist, Lady Playing the Kithara*, c 50 BC, fresco. Metropolitan Museum of Art, New York

4 Anonymous Egyptian Artist, *Ladies Listening to a Harpist*, 20th Dynasty (c 1000 BC) tempera on plaster. Valley of the Nobles, Thebes

2

1

3

4

5

5 Jan Vermeer, *Girl with a Guitar*, 1670, oil on canvas. Iveagh Bequest, Kenwood House, London

6 Edouard Manet, *Music at the Tuileries Garden*, 1862, oil on canvas. National Gallery, London

6

DANCE

1 Pierre-Auguste Renoir, *La Moulin de la Galette*, 1876, oil on canvas. John Hay Whitney Collection, New York

2 Henri Gaudier-Brezska, *Red Stone Dancer*, c 1913, Red Mansfield stone. Tate Gallery, London

3 Eva Roos, *Impromptu Ball*, c 1894, oil on canvas. Private Collection

1

2

3

4

4 Anonymous Mughal Artist, *Two Girls Performing Kathak Dance*, c 1675, watercolour. Victoria and Albert Museum, London

5 Henri de Toulouse-Lautrec, *Dance at the Moulin Rouge*, 1892, oil on cardboard. Narodni Muzeum, Prague

5

THEATRE

1 Pierre-Auguste Renoir, *La Première Sortie,* c 1880, oil on canvas. National Gallery, London

2 Edgar Degas, *Theatre Scene,* c 1875, pastel. Private Collection

3 Edgar Degas, *Café Concert at the Ambassadeurs,* 1876–7, pastel. Musée des Beaux Arts, Lyons

4 Spencer Gore, *Box at the Theatre,* c 1912, oil on canvas. Anthony D'Offay Gallery, London

1

2

3

4

5

6

5 Septimus Scott, *Ballet,* c 1895, lithograph. A. & F. Pears Ltd, London

6 Antoine Watteau, *Commedia dell'Arte,* c 1715, oil on canvas. National Gallery of Art, Washington

7 Eva Gonzalès, *A Box at the Italians' Theatre,* 1874, oil on canvas. Musée d'Orsay, Paris

7

CIRCUS

1 Edgar Degas,
La La at the Circus,
1879, oil on canvas.
National Gallery,
London

1

2

2 Ernst Ludwig Kirchner, *Acrobats,* c 1920, oil on canvas. Private Collection

3 Kitagawa Utamaro, *A Monkey Trainer,* 1788, woodblock print. Private Collection

3

PICNICS

1 Giorgione or Titian, *Fête Champêtre,* 1509–15, oil on canvas. Louvre, Paris

2 Edouard Manet, *Le Déjeuner sur l'herbe,* 1863, oil on canvas. Louvre, Paris

1

2

3

4

3 Jean-Honoré Fragonard, *The Swing,* c 1775, oil on canvas. Kress Collection Washington DC

4 James Tissot, *The Picnic,* 1881–2, oil on panel. Musée de Dijon

GAMES

1 Anonymous Japanese Artist, *Children at Play,* screen, 18c, watercolour on paper. Private Collection

2 Jan Steen, *A Country Inn with Skittle Players,* c 1660, oil on canvas. Private Collection

1

2

3 Pieter Bruegel the Elder, *Children's Games,* 1560, oil on panel. Kunsthistorisches Museum, Vienna

3

HOME LIFE

1 Paul Signac, *Woman with a Lamp,* 1890, oil on canvas. Musée d'Orsay, Paris

2 Mangetsudo, *Young Girl Adjusting her Hair in a Mirror,* 1750s, woodblock print. British Museum, London

3 Jan Vermeer, *Girl Reading a Letter by an Open Window,* c 1660, oil on canvas. Gemäldegalerie, Dresden

4 Berthe Morisot, *Hortensia,* 1894, oil on canvas. Musée d'Orsay, Paris

1

2

3

4

5

5 Mary Cassatt, *Reading the Figaro,* 1883, oil on canvas. Private Collection

6 Paul Cézanne, *Madame Cézanne Sewing,* c 1877, oil on canvas. Private Collection

7 Jean-Honoré Fragonard, *The Billet-Doux,* 1780s, oil on canvas. Metropolitan Musuem of Art, New York

6

7

SPORT

1 Anonymous French Artist, *Preparing Nets for Hunting,* c 1390, watercolour. Bibliothèque Nationale, Paris

2 Edouard Manet, *Bullfight,* c 1866, oil on canvas. Private Collection

3 Edouard Manet, *Races at Longchamp,* 1861, oil on canvas. Private Collection

1

3

2

4 Anonymous, *Maximilian I Hunting Deer,* for a Tyrolese Hunt Book c 1510, oil and tempera on glass. Bibliothèque Royale, Brussels

5 Anonymous Mughal Artist, *A Game of Polo,* mid 17c, watercolour. Victoria and Albert Museum, London

4

5

6 Anonymous Mughal Artist, *A Wrestler Stretching a Bow,* early 18c, watercolour. Victoria and Albert Museum, London

7 Nikosthenes, *Boxers and Wrestlers,* c 550–525 BC, black figure, neck amphora. British Museum, London

8 Simon Benning, *Killing the Boar,* c 1540, watercolour on vellum. British Library, London

9 Gabrielle Bella, *Game of Racquets,* early 18c, oil on panel. Galleria Querini-Stampalia, Venice

6

7

8

9

10

10 Spencer Gore, *Game of Tennis,* c 1908, oil on canvas. Roy Miles Fine Paintings, London

11 Anonymous Mughal Artist, *Prince Salim Surprised by a Lion while Hunting,* c 1600, watercolour. Private Collection

11

BY THE RIVER

1 George Seurat, *The Bathers Asnieres,* 1883–4, oil on canvas. National Gallery, London

2 Edouard Manet, *Argenteuil,* 1874, oil on canvas. Musée des Beaux Arts, Tournai

3 Alfred Sisley, *Regatta at Molesey,* 1874, oil on canvas. Musée d'Orsay, Paris

4 Edouard Manet, *Boating,* 1874, oil on canvas. Metropolitan Museum of Art, New York

1

2

3

4

5

5 George Seurat, *Sunday Afternoon on the Grand Jatte,* 1884–6, oil on canvas. Art Institute of Chicago

6

6 Anonymous Flemish Artist, *Boating in May,* early 16c, watercolour. British Library, London

BEACHES

1 Claude Monet, *The Beach at Trouville,* 1870, oil on canvas. National Gallery, London

2 Richard Parkes Bonington, *French Coastal Scene,* 1820s, oil on canvas. Art Gallery, Wolverhampton

1

2

3

3 Peter Severin Kroyer, *Summer Evening on the Skagen, Southern Beach with Anna Ancher and Maria Kroyer,* 1893, oil on canvas. Skagens Museum, Denmark

4 Eugène Boudin, *The Beach,* 1867, oil on canvas. Private Collection

4

AT HOME

Paintings tell us an enormous amount about how some people lived in the past, the furniture they used, how they decorated their rooms, what utensils they used on their tables, what they ate, how they cooked and how they slept, but they do this in quite different ways. Flemish artists using oil paint created a tradition of meticulous depiction, while Japanese and Indian artists were adept at multiple viewpoints which enabled them to show both exteriors and interiors in the same picture. In Kalan and Dharmadas' commemorative watercolour of the *Birth of Prince Salim* we see simultaneously the whole palace from the outside to the intimacy of the birth within the harem. Medieval European artists, preferring a single viewpoint, often showed an interior as if one of the walls had been removed, making it look like a kind of static, ceremonial theatre. Sometimes, the setting is a physical impossibility, like that in Antonello's *St Jerome in his Study*, with his attendant lion, in a strange building which looks like a gothic church without side walls, or Botticelli's marriage feast set in a half-complete classical architectural fantasy in a garden.

Until the sixteenth century, painting tells us little about how the poor lived, except in scenes like the birth of Christ in a stable or episodes from the lives of saints like St Francis who took vows of poverty. Until then most pictures tell us only about the houses of the rich, particularly the great ceremonial halls in which they received and entertained guests.

Bedrooms and bed scenes figure widely in painting since the three most profound events in life (birth, copulation and death), tend to take place in bed. Scenes like the birth of the Virgin portrayed the intimate secrets of patrician ladies' bedrooms, while Carpaccio's rather prosaic depiction of *Dream of St Ursula* came to symbolize to Ruskin his own rather melancholy and sexless honeymoon. Quite different in every way is Rembrandt's intimate view of his plump young mistress, *Hendrique Stoffels in Bed*, painted in haste, charged with sensuality, anticipation and pleasure.

During the Renaissance the new ideal of the scholarly life was often expressed as a scene showing one of the doctors of the church, working in a Humanist's book-lined room. Manet was echoing that tradition when he painted *Emile Zola in his Study*.

Renaissance grandees, inspired by descriptions of Roman collections and palaces, also began to build picture and sculpture galleries in which to display their collections of Roman marbles and Italian paintings, emblems of their wealth, taste and sophistication. Likewise an eighteenth-century dilettante such as George Towneley chose to be depicted in his Gallery surrounded by his classical marbles and forgeries.

Pictures such as these, however, did not have much of a market in Dutch middle-class homes, and painters like de Hooch, Steen and Vermeer represented more mundane and bourgeois preoccupations. Their pictures remind us too that, until the nineteenth century, crafts like carpentry and weaving were carried on in the home. Even wealthy merchants like *George Grisze* and *Constantijn Huygens* worked in their homes. Only in the nineteenth century did men begin to leave the home entirely to their wives, and society painters like Tissot and Grimshaw turned bourgeois luxury into a chocolate-box genre.

By contrast, the poor led more intimate, crowded and miserable lives, though the conditions in which they struggled to survive were often prettified by minor painters. Van Gogh's early work, *The Potato Eaters*, derives its potency from his determination to depict the life of the poor in all its grimy, hungry, dark essentials.

Kesu Kalan and Dharmadas, *Birth of Prince Salim*, c 1590, watercolour. Victoria and Albert Museum, London

Still life painting emerged in Europe as a distinct genre in sixteenth-century Holland. Originally such pictures had clear symbolic meanings; bread and wine signified the Christian sacrament; precious books and jewels symbolized the vanity and mortality of earthly things. But soon pictures of flowers, dead animals, fruit, musical instruments, books and jewels became decorations themselves in the houses of the wealthy bourgeois throughout Europe. It is some measure of the strange genius of Chardin that he was able to transform such a superficial genre and elevate still life to the status of academic acceptance: *The Skate* won him entry to the French Academy.

AFFLUENCE

1 Anonymous Portuguese Artist, *The Last Supper*, 15c, oil on panel. National Museum of Ancient Art, Lisbon

2 Gianbattista Tiepolo, *The Banquet of Anthony and Cleopatra*, c 1750, fresco. Palazzo Labia, Venice

3 Anonymous Flemish Artist, *Court of Alexander the Great* (detail), c 1470–80, watercolour. British Library, London

1

2

3

4

4 Antonello da Messina, *St Jerome in his Study*, c 1475, oil on panel. National Gallery, London

5 Daniel Mytens, *Earl of Arundel in his Study*, c 1618, oil on canvas. Arundel Castle, Sussex

6 Anonymous French School, *Gabrielle d'Estrées in her Bath*, early 17c, oil on canvas. Musée Condé, Chantilly

5

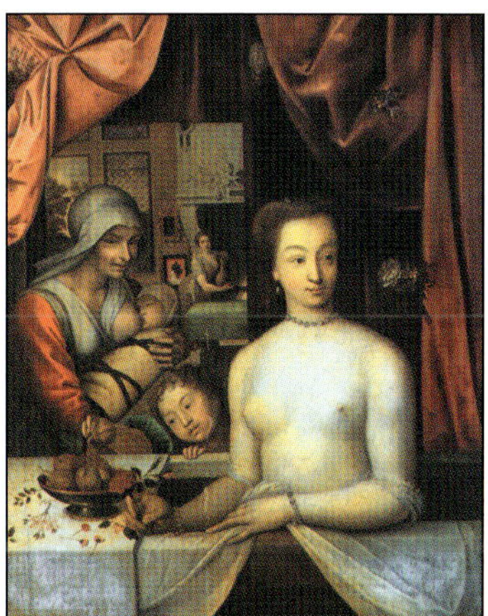

6

7 Sandro Botticelli, *The Wedding Feast*, 1483, tempera on panel. Watney Collection, Charlbury, Oxfordshire

8 Artoro Ricci, *The Game of Chess*, 1880, oil on canvas. Private Collection

9 Johann Zoffany, *Charles Towneley in his Gallery*, 1781, oil on canvas. Towneley Hall Museum and Art Gallery, Burnley

7

8

9

10 Vittore Carpaccio, *St Augustine in his Study*, 1502–8, fresco. Scuola di S Giorgio degli Schiavoni, Venice

10

11 David Teniers the Younger, *Archduke Leopold-Wilhelm's Studio*, 1651, oil on canvas. Petworth House, Sussex

11

BEDROOMS

1 Anonymous German Artist, *Tobias and Sarah in bed*, 16c, stained glass. Victoria and Albert Museum

2 Anonymous Indian Artist, *Lovers in Bed*, 18c, watercolour. Victor Lownes Collection, London

3 Cologne School, *The Annunciation*, early 16c, oil on panel. Musée des Beaux Arts, Lille

4 Vincent van Gogh, *His Bedroom in Arles*, 1889, oil on canvas. Musée d'Orsay, Paris

1

3

2

4

5

5 Rembrandt, *Hendrijke Stoffels in Bed*, 1647, oil on canvas. National Gallery of Scotland, Edinburgh

6 School of the Veneto, *The Birth of the Virgin*, c 1480, tempera on panel. Private Collection

7 Vittore Carpaccio, *Dream of St Ursula*, 1490–6, tempera on panel. Accademia, Venice

6

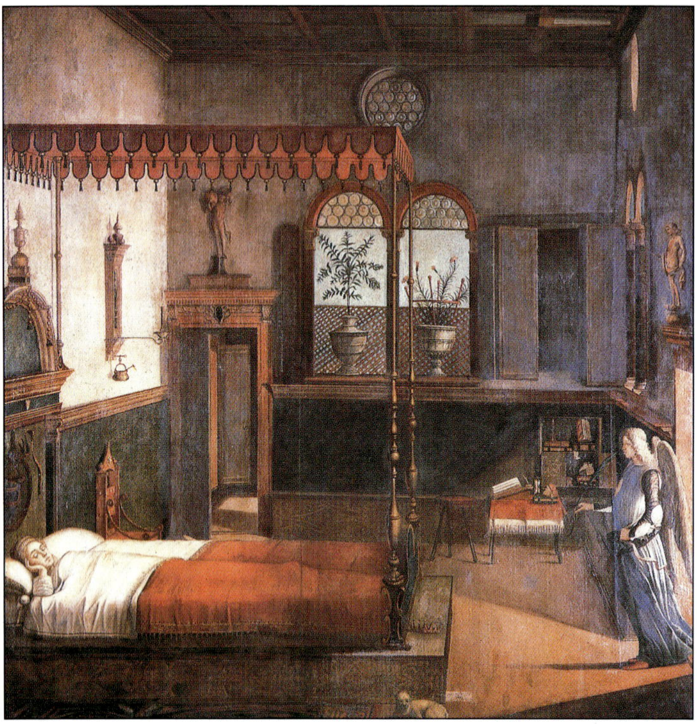

7

1

2

3

4

KITCHENS

1 Jan Bruegel, *The Distinguished Visitor*, c 1600, oil on canvas. Kunsthistorisches Museum, Vienna

2 Joachim Bueckelaer, *Interior of a Kitchen*, c 1570, oil on canvas. Louvre, Paris

3 Willem van Herp, *A Woman in her Kitchen Interior*, 1660s, oil on canvas. Johnny van Haeften Gallery, London

4 Adriaen van Utrecht, *A Kitchen*, c 1620, oil on canvas. Private Collection

BOURGEOIS LIFE

1 Thomas de Keyser, *Constantijn Huygens and his Clerk*, 1627, oil on canvas. National Gallery, London

2 Jan Steen, *Grace before Meat*, c 1660, oil on canvas. Belvoir Castle, Leicestershire

3 Pieter de Hooch, *A Woman and her Maid*, c 1660, oil on canvas. National Gallery, London

4 William Hogarth, *Shortly After the Marriage,*"plate 2 from *Marriage à la Mode*, 1743–5, oil on canvas. National Gallery, London

1

2

3

4

5

5 Vilhelm Hammershoi, *A Woman Sewing*, c 1900, oil on canvas. Private Collection

6

6 Atkinson Grimshaw, *Summer*, 1875, oil on canvas. Roy Miles Fine Paintings, London

POVERTY

1

1 Jean-François Clermont, *Peasants in their Cottage*, c 1780, oil on canvas. Private Collection

2

2 Vincent van Gogh, *The Potato Eaters*, 1885, oil on canvas. Stedelijk Museum, Amsterdam

3 Georges de La Tour, *Woman with a Flea*, c 1635, oil on canvas. Musée des Beaux Arts, Nancy

4 Rembrandt, *The Carpenter's Household*, 1640, oil on wood. Louvre, Paris

3

4

STILL LIFE

1 Cornelis Kruys, *Still Life*, c 1655, oil on canvas. Johnny van Haeften Gallery, London

2 Jean-Baptiste Chardin, *The Skate*, 1728, oil on canvas. Louvre, Paris

3 Pieter van Roestraeten, *A Vanitas – Still Life*, c 1660, oil on canvas. Private Collection

1

2

3

4

5

4 Jean-Baptiste Chardin, *The Copper Urn*, c 1734, oil on canvas. Louvre, Paris

5 Goya, *Still Life, a Butcher's Counter*, c 1800, oil on canvas. Louvre, Paris

CITIES

Roman artists often depicted cityscapes as decorations for patrician villas, creating the illusion of a window onto the world outside. Medieval artists, when illustrating stories and histories about cities they had never seen, often chose to paint them as if they were not different from those of their own world. A view of Paris might serve for a view of London, Rome or Heidelberg. Thus the anonymous *View of Jerusalem* tells us a lot about the fifteenth-century European townscape, but nothing about Jerusalem. The view in *Marco Polo Leaving Venice for China* was probably painted by an artist who had never seen the city and who had to base his invention on written descriptions and other artists' conventionalized depictions of it. In certain cases the view is clearly both idealized and based on the motifs of the city concerned. *The Tower of London with London Bridge Behind*, for instance, suggests that the artist had actually looked at the city but from an impossible imaginary viewpoint.

By the sixteenth century, however, with the increase in trade and European conquest, pictures of exotic and unknown cultures, like White's view of *The Town of Pomeioc* or the Spanish painting of the Aztec capital *Mexico City*, depicted aspects of foreign cultures which could never be conveyed by words. When Europeans first began to trade in Japan and the East they provided a market for local painters. Japanese townscapes and landscapes were brought back in large quantities and in turn influenced European taste.

The expansion of the European world system meant that ports expanded rapidly in size and importance. *Bristol Broad Quay* and *Lisbon Harbour* show these two cities grown rich on the profits of the slave trade, and wealthy cities like London and Amsterdam acted as magnets for artists and for buyers, both local and foreign. By the eighteenth century the distinctive character of each city was quite widely commented on, and the increase in foreign travel created a market for pictures of those most visited, for example, Rome, because of its historical and religious associations, and Venice, because of its exotic role as the gateway to the Orient. English lords became avid collectors of such pictures and crammed their houses with these mementos of their travels. Canaletto, possibly the greatest of all topographical artists, had a profound influence on the genre, and his pictures of Rome, Venice and London greatly influenced the ways in which subsequent artists and imitators depicted those cities, while artists like Pannini concentrated on monuments such as the Pantheon for which there was an almost insatiable demand.

Hogarth's great cycles of paintings, *A Rake's Progress* and *Marriage à la Mode*, create a vivid and detailed impression of the vices of the great metropolis, while another series, *The Four Times of Day*, gives a perspective on the lives of the poor and dispossessed, normally excluded from high art. Of all cities, however, it is Paris which has played the greatest role in the evolution of modern art, and hardly surprisingly, pictures of Paris and Parisian life can be found throughout this book, whether Seurat's depictions of suburban leisure resorts, Manet's street scenes or the cityscapes of Monet, Pissarro and Sisley. The anonymity and alienation of modern urban existence is graphically portrayed by artists as different as Munch, Kirchner and Boccioni.

Anonymous Roman Artist, *Villa Decoration* at Boscoreale, Pompeii, 1c BC, fresco. Metropolitan Museum of Art, New York

TOWNS

1 John White, *The Town of Pomeioc, Virginia*, 1585–6, watercolour. British Museum, London

2 David Cox, *Hay on Wye,* c 1835, watercolour. British Museum, London

1

2

3

3 Albrecht Dürer, *A Castle Courtyard, Innsbruck*, 1494, watercolour. Albertina, Vienna

4 Richard Parkes Bonington, *La Place du Molard, Geneva*, c 1807, watercolour. British Museum, London

5 Barend Gael, *Poultry Market by a Church*, c 1650, oil on canvas. Johnny van Haeften Gallery, London

6 Anonymous Japanese Artist, *European Traders in Nagasaki*, late 18c, watercolour scroll. Private Collection

4

6

5

7 Gillis Mostaert, *A View of Hoboken, near Antwerp*, 1583, oil on canvas. Private Collection

8 Jan Bruegel the Elder, *A Village Market*, 1613, oil on canvas. Private Collection

7

8

EARLY CITIES

1 Anonymous, *View of Jerusalem*, c 1435, watercolour. British Museum, London

2

3

4

5

2 Anonymous, *Marco Polo Leaving Venice for China*, c 1400, watercolour. Bodleian Library, Oxford

3 Anonymous, *Feudal Nobility outside Paris*, c 1390, watercolour. Bibliothèque Nationale, Paris

4 Anonymous French Artist, *The Tower of London with London Bridge Behind*, c 1500, manuscript. British Library, London

5 Jean Fouquet, *View of the Ile de la Cité, Paris*, c 1450, watercolour. Bibliothèque Nationale, Paris

6 Anonymous Japanese Artist, *A View of Kyoto*, 17c, screen painting. Private Collection

7 Anonymous Tosa School Artist, *A View of Kyoto*, c 1800, ink, bodycolour and gold. Victoria and Albert Museum, London

8 Anonymous Spanish Artist, *Mexico City*, 17c, watercolour. British Library, London

9 Anonymous Florentine Artist, *View of Florence*, c 1500, tempera on panel. Private Collection

6

7

8

9

PORTS

1

2

3

1 Anonymous English Artist, *Bristol, Broad Quay,* c 1730, oil on canvas. City Art Gallery, Bristol

2 Peter Monamy, *Lisbon Harbour,* c 1730, oil on canvas. Oscar and Peter Johnson Ltd, London

3 Gerrit Berckheyde, *Canal View in Amsterdam,* 1685, oil on canvas. Johnny van Haeften Gallery, London

4 Heinrich Hansen, *Copenhagen,* 1887, oil on canvas. Private Collection

5 Anonymous, *View of Canton,* c 1825, oil on panel. Private Collection

6 Antonio Joli, *View of Naples,* c 1750, oil on canvas. Private Collection

4

5

6

7

8

9

7 Edmund Niemann, *Whitby,* 1850, oil on canvas. Oscar and Peter Johnson Ltd, London

8 Samuel Prout, *View of a Fishing Village,* c 1806, watercolour. Victoria and Albert Museum, London

9 Camille Pissarro, *Great Bridge at Rouen,* 1896, oil on canvas. Carnegie Institute, Museum of Arts, Pittsburg

LONDON

1

2

3

4

5

1 Anonymous "AS", *An Early London Coffee House*, 1668, watercolour. British Museum, London

2 William Hogarth, *The Four Times of Day, Morning (Covent Garden)*, 1736–7, oil on canvas. Private Collection

3 Antonio Canaletto, *The Thames and the City of London from Richmond House*, 1746, oil on canvas. Private Collection

4 Walter Greaves, *Unloading the Barges, Looking towards Battersea Church*, c 1860, oil on canvas. Kensington and Chelsea Public Library, London

5 Camille Pissarro, *The Crystal Palace, Sydenham*, 1871, oil on canvas. Art Institute of Chicago

6

7

8

6 Atkinson Grimshaw, *The Pool and London Bridge at Night*, 1884, oil on canvas. Private Collection

7 J. O'Connor, *St Pancras Hotel and Pentonville Road*, 1884, oil on canvas. Museum of London

8 André Derain, *Pool of London*, 1906, oil on canvas. Tate Gallery, London

VENICE

1 Vittore Carpaccio, *The Miracle of the Relic of the True Cross – the Grand Canal, Venice*, c 1495, tempera on panel. Accademia, Venice

2 Antonio Canaletto, *The Grand Canal, Venice*, c 1760, oil on canvas. Private Collection

3 Antonio Canaletto, *Carnivale* (detail), c 1756, oil on canvas. Bowes Museum, Barnard Castle, Durham

4 J.M.W. Turner, *Venice Looking East from the Giudecca*, 1840, watercolour. British Museum, London

1

2

3

4

5

6

5 Camille Corot, *Piazzetta, Venice*, 1834, oil on canvas. Louvre, Paris

6 Edouard Manet, *The Grand Canal,* 1875, oil on canvas. Provident Securities Company, San Francisco

ROME

1 Giovanni Paolo Pannini, *The Interior of the Pantheon, Rome*, c 1720, oil on canvas. Private Collection

2 Bernardo Bellotto, *Castel St Angelo and San Giovanni dei Fiorentini, Rome*, c 1745, oil on canvas. Private Collection

3 Camille Corot, *The Castel St Angelo*, 1843, oil on canvas. Musée des Beaux Arts, Lille

1

2

3

4

5

6

4 David Roberts, *The Forum in Rome*, 1859, oil on canvas. Guildhall Art Gallery, London

5 Antonio Canaletto, *Colosseum and the Arch of Constantine, Rome*, c 1720, oil on canvas. Private Collection

6 Umberto Boccioni, *Workshops at the Porta Romana*, 1908, oil on canvas. Banca Italiana Commerciale, Milan

PARIS

1 Jean Béraud, *Outside the Théâtre du Vaudeville, Paris*, c 1890, oil on canvas. Musée Carnavalet, Paris

1

DE LA LOCATION
SYLVIE

2 Jean Béraud, *Gloppe's Patisserie on the Champs Elysées,* 1889, oil on canvas. Musée Carnavalet, Paris

3 Claude Monet, *St Lazare Station,* 1877, oil on canvas. Musée d'Orsay, Paris

2

3

4

4 Camille Pissarro, *Le Boulevard Montmartre*, 1893, oil on canvas. Private Collection

5

5 Claude Monet, *Boulevard des Capucines*, 1873, oil on canvas. Pushkin Museum, Moscow

LANDSCAPES

We have seen in the earlier chapters that elements of landscape painting are often present in the depiction of genre subjects like work and leisure. In Egyptian art, however, trees, plants and water were always conventionalized and the celebration of the beauty and delights of nature only became common in Greek and Roman pastoral poetry. Catering for this new kind of sensitivity Roman artists often depicted *trompe l'oeil* landscapes to decorate the walls of patrician villas.

In post-classical art, landscape elements again were pushed into the background, but in medieval France, Flanders and England landscape became one of the major elements in illuminated manuscripts. Although artists like Leonardo and Dürer filled sketchbooks with exquisite landscape studies, these were essentially preparatory studies for the backgrounds to their paintings. At this time watercolour became increasingly popular because it facilitated the making of quick sketches on the spot.

Altdorfer appears to have been the first European artist to paint landscape as a subject in its own right. During the sixteenth century, Flemish artists turned increasingly to landscape, often depicting views with greatly exaggerated features, impossible mountains, cataracts and forests. By the seventeenth century a more naturalistic mode was developed in the work of Flemish artists like Rubens and Dutch artists like Hobbema. At the same time the conventions of the ideal or classical landscape were elaborated in sixteenth-century Rome by French artists like Claude and Poussin.

Eighteenth-century England saw a rapid development of these two traditions. Artists like Wilson took the formulas of Claude and applied them to quite different subjects, while the "picturesque" notions of landscape were developed by amateurs like Gilpin and professionals like Cozens and Gainsborough. Watercolour as a medium was increasingly used in England, as can be seen in the work of Girtin, Cotman and Turner. Turner, however, although brought up in the 'picturesque' tradition, evolved a more symbolic, romantic mode with his studies of avalanches, cataracts and storms, and in his later masterpieces the subject matter has all but dissolved in a swirling vortex which simulates the blinding effects of light.

Friedrich, Turner's great German contemporary, introduced something quite new into the genre; sunrise, dusk and moonlight, bathing the scene with a uniform light, created spiritual and philosophical meanings in landscape, and his painting of ice, snow, mist, moonlight and ruined buildings introduced a mysterious element into European art.

Parallels to this mystical contemplation of nature can be seen in Chinese and Japanese art, especially in the work of Hiroshige and Tessan where long-established Buddhist and poetic traditions gave landscapes a quite different character and meaning.

Constable's technique evolved slowly and it was only at the end of his life that his originality of vision and technique began to be appreciated. When *The Hay Wain* was exhibited in Paris, it stimulated Delacroix to alter his technique, and Constable's attempt to exclude poetic and literary associations form his art also influenced nineteenth-century French painters like Corot. His realism had an indirect influence on Courbet as well.

It was the Impressionists, however, who raised landscape to the popular status it now enjoys. Monet's landscapes introduced something quite new, although earlier painters like Constable, Turner and Bonington

Albrecht Altdorfer, *Landscape with Church,* c 1511, ink and watercolour. Albertina, Vienna

had also painted in the open air. Monet's fidelity to his subject was taken even further, and he often produced dozens of variants on haystacks, poplars, waterlilies and so on. Cézanne's ambition to uncover the underlying order of nature forced him to rework his pictures for years, while van Gogh attempted to capture the emotional and expressive essentials of a scene in a single session. His conviction that the art of the future would be an art of colour influenced many later painters, as did Gauguin's decision to leave Europe in search of the rich, exotic civilizations and landscapes of the Pacific.

LIGHT & NIGHT

1 Caspar David Friedrich, *Easter Morning*, c 1815, oil on canvas. Private collection

2 Atkinson Grimshaw, *After the Shower,* c 1880, oil on canvas. Christopher Wood Gallery, London

3 Utogawa Hiroshige, *Kyoto Bridge by Moonlight,* c 1855, woodblock print. Victoria and Albert Museum, London

1

2

3

4

5

6

7

4 Claude Monet, *Impression – Sunrise,* 1872, oil on canvas. Musée Marmottan, Paris

5 Gustave Courbet, *L'Immensité,* c 1870, oil on canvas. Victoria and Albert Museum, London

6 Joseph Wright, *Cromford Mill by Moonlight,* c 1783, oil on canvas. Private Collection

7 Philip de Loutherbourg, *Coalbrookdale by Night,* 1801, oil on canvas. Science Museum, London

8 Caspar David Friedrich, *Remembrance of Johann Bremer,* c 1817, oil on canvas. Schloss Charlottenberg, Berlin

9 J.M.W. Turner, *Sun Setting over a Lake,* 1840–5, oil on canvas. Tate Gallery, London

8

9

1

2

CLASSICAL

1 Claude Lorraine, *Landscape with Arrival of Aeneas at Pallanteum*, 1675, oil on canvas. National Trust, Anglesea

2 Nicolas Poussin, *Orpheus and Eurydice,* c 1650, oil on canvas. Louvre, Paris

PICTURESQUE

1 John Sell Cotman, *Landscape with River and Cattle*, c 1803, watercolour. Victoria and Albert Museum, London

2 John Constable, *Trees and a Stretch of Water on the Stour*, 1836–7, ink wash. Victoria and Albert Museum, London

1

2

3

3 William Gilpin, *Landscape, The Wye Valley?* c 1770, pen and ink wash. Victoria and Albert Museum, London

4 Thomas Gainsborough, *Cowherd in a Landscape,* c 1785, oil on canvas. Private Collection on loan to City Art Gallery, York

4

WORKING THE LAND

1 Anonymous English Artist, *The Harvest in Dixton, Gloucestershire*, c 1780, oil on canvas. Art Gallery and Museum, Cheltenham

2 Anonymous English Artist, *The Slate Quarry,* c 1780, oil on canvas. Cider House Galleries Ltd, Bletchingley, Surrey

1

2

3

3 George Robert Lewis, *Harvest Scene, Hereford, Dynedor and the Malvern Hills from the Haywood Lodge,* 1815, oil on canvas. Tate Gallery, London

NATURAL SCENES

1

1 Vincent van Gogh, *Le Crau, Peach Trees in Blossom,* 1889, oil on canvas. Courtauld Institute Galleries, London

2

2 Gustave Courbet, *The Oak of Vercingetorix,* c 1860, oil on canvas. Pennsylvania Academy of Fine Arts, Philadelphia

3

4

3 Albrecht Dürer, *The Great Piece of Turf*, 1502, watercolour. Albertina, Vienna

4 Richard Burchet, *Cornfield, Isle of Wight*, c 1850, oil on canvas. Victoria and Albert Museum, London

5 Camille Corot, *The Village of Avray*, c 1840, oil on canvas. Louvre, Paris

6 Albrecht Altdorfer, *Landscape with Footbridge*, c 1520, oil on paper. National Gallery, London

7 Paul Cézanne, *The Gulf of Marseilles*, 1883–5, oil on canvas. Louvre, Paris

8 Richard Wilson, *Cader Idris*, c 1774, oil on canvas. Tate Gallery, London

5

6

7

8

9

9 Meindert Hobbema, *Avenue of Trees*, 1689, oil on canvas. National Gallery, London

10 John Constable, *The Hay Wain*, 1821, oil on canvas. National Gallery, London

10

FANTASTIC

1 Benozzo Gozzoli, *The Journey of the Magi,* 1459, fresco. Palazzo Medici Riccardi, Florence

2 Monogrammist of Brunswick, *The Sacrifice of Isaac by Abraham,* 1550s, oil on canvas. Louvre, Paris

1

2

3

4

3 Paul Bril, *A Fantastic Landscape*, c 1600, oil on glass. Johnny van Haeften Gallery, London

4 Henri Rousseau, *The Snake Charmer*, 1907, oil on canvas. Musée d'Orsay, Paris

5 Lucas van Gassel, *The Flight into Egypt*, c 1550, oil on canvas. Johnny van Haeften Gallery, London

6 Giovanni Bellini, *Agony in the Garden*, c 1459, tempera on panel. National Gallery, London

5

6

EXOTIC LANDS

1 Mori Shushin Tessan, *Deer and Maple Tree*, c 1810, woodblock print. British Museum, London

1

2

2 Ando Hiroshige, *Wisteria in Full Bloom*, c 1857, woodblock print. British Museum, London

3 Anonymous Kangra Artist, *Rada and Krishna Walking in a Grove*, 1820–25, watercolour. Victoria and Albert Museum, London

4 Ando Hiroshige, *Maple Leaves at the Tekoyna Shrine*, 1857, woodblock print. British Museum, London

3

4

5 Hubert Settler, *A Hilly Landscape in Palestine*, 1846, oil on canvas. Private Collection

6 Edward Lear, *Philae on the Nile*, 1850, watercolour. Private Collection

5

6

THE NEW FRONTIER

1

1 Jackson Pollock, *Going West*, 1934–8, oil on panel. Smithsonian Institute, Washington DC

2

2 Thomas Moran, *Grand Canyon of the Yellowstone River,* 1872, oil on canvas. United States Department of the Interior, Washington DC

3

3 Thomas Cole, *The Last of the Mohicans,* c 1830, oil on canvas. New York State Historical Society

4

4 Charles Wimar, *The Attack on the Emigrant Train,* 1856, oil on canvas. University of Michigan Museum of Art

WATER

1 William Turner, *Cherwell Waterlilies*, c 1850, watercolour. Royal Society of Watercolour, London

2 Charles-François Daubigny, *The Lock at Opteroz*, 1853, oil on canvas. Musée des Beaux Arts, Rouen

3 Albrecht Dürer, *House on the Pond*, c 1495–7, watercolour. British Museum, London

4 Camille Pissarro, *The Flood at Eragny*, 1893, oil on canvas. Private Collection

1

2

3

4

5

5 Katsushika Hokusai, *In the Well of the Great Wave at Kangawa*, 1834–5, woodblock print. Private Collection

6

6 Paul Gauguin, *The Beach at Poldu*, 1889, oil on canvas. Private Collection

7 Thomas Girtin, *The White House, Chelsea*, 1800, watercolour. Tate Gallery, London

8 William Alexander, *The Emperor of China's Gardens*, 1793, watercolour. Imperial Palace, Peking

9 James Whaite, *A Picnic on the Coast, Isle of Wight*, watercolour. Private Collection

7

8

9

10

10 Alfred Sisley, *La Berge à Ste Mammes*, 1890, oil on canvas. Private Collection

11 Katsushika Hokusai, *The Waterfall at Yoshuio*, c 1830, woodblock print. Harari Collection, London

12 John Sell Cotman, *Chirk Aqueduct*, c 1803–4, watercolour. Victoria and Albert Museum, London

11

12

STORMS

1 Peter Paul Rubens, *Landscape with Philemon and Baucis*, 1620s, oil on panel. Kunshistorisches Museum, Vienna

2 Gakutei, *Sudden Rain on Mount Tempo*, 1834, woodblock print. British Museum, London

3 John Robert Cozens, *View of a Castle between Bolzano and Trent*, c 1783, watercolour. Victoria and Albert Museum, London

4 J.M.W. Turner, *Travellers in a Snowdrift on Mount Tarrar*, 1829, watercolour. British Museum, London

1

2

3

4

5

5 Giorgione, *The Tempest*, 1503, oil on canvas. Accademia, Venice

6 J.M.W. Turner, *Hannibal Crossing the Alps*, 1812, oil on canvas. Tate Gallery, London

6

GARDENS

1 Hippolyte Petitjean, *The Orchard under the Snow*, c 1890, oil on canvas. Private Collection

2 Claude Monet, *Spring at Giverny*, c 1905, oil on canvas. Private Collection

1

2

3

4

5

6

3 Camille Pissarro, *Kitchen Garden and Trees in Blossom, Pontoise*, c 1872, oil on canvas. Musée d'Orsay, Paris

4 John Constable, *Golding Constable's Flower Garden*, 1815, oil on canvas. Ipswich Museum, Suffolk

5 Albert Goodwin, *Pleasant Land*, 1875, watercolour. Victoria and Albert Museum, London

6 Oskar Bergman, *A View of Gotland, Sweden*, c 1910, gouache. Private Collection

7 Pierre-Auguste Renoir, *La Serre*, c 1900, oil on canvas. Private Collection

8 George Dunlop Leslie, *Five O'Clock*, c 1890, oil on canvas. Forbes Magazine Collection, New York

7

8

9

10

11

9 Walter Crane, *Madonna Lilies in a Garden*, 1908, oil on canvas. Private Collection

10 Claude Monet, *Garden at Vétheuil*, 1881, oil on canvas. Private Collection

11 Claude Monet, *The Terrace at St Andresse*, 1867, oil on canvas. Metropolitan Museum of Art, New York

12 Edward Calvert, *The Primitive City*, 1822, watercolour. Private Collection

13 Anonymous Mughal Artist, *Rustam in a Garden*, c 1565, watercolour. Victoria and Albert Museum, London

14 Hugo van der Goes, *The Fall*, c 1470, oil on panel. Kunshistorisches Museum, Vienna

15 Gunakati Ragini, *A Lady Attending Two Potted Plants*, c 1680, watercolour. Victoria and Albert Museum, London

16 Anonymous Roman Artist, *Landscape Decoration* of a villa at Boscoreale, Pompeii c 20 BC, fresco. Metropolitan Museum of Art, New York

12

13

14

15

16

17

18

19

20

17 Pierre-Denis Martin, *The Orangery at Versailles*, 1720s, oil on canvas. Château, Versailles

18 Anonymous Flemish Painter, *Garden with a Tennis Court and Biblical Scenes of David and Bathsheba*, mid 16c, oil on panel. MCC, London

19 Jacob Grimmer, *The Spring*, c 1650, oil on panel. Musée des Beaux Arts, Lille

20 William Havell, *Garden Scene in Rio de Janeiro*, 1827, watercolour. Victoria and Albert Museum, London

FLOWERS

1 Odilon Redon, *Vase of Blue Flowers*, c 1905–8, pastel. Private Collection

2 Ogata Korin, *Irises*, c 1700, watercolour on a screen. Nezu Art Museum, Tokyo

1

2

3

3 Christopher Wood, *Flowers in a Pot*, c 1925, oil on canvas. Private Collection

4 Nakamura Hochu, *Flowers of the Seasons*, panel of Japanese screen, ink and colour on gold, c 1800. British Museum, London

5 Anonymous American Artist, *Flowers and Fruit*, mid 19c, oil on canvas. National Gallery of Art, Washington, DC

4

5

6 Jan van Os, *Flowers in an Urn with Fruit and a Bird's Nest on a Marble Plinth*, c 1780, oil on canvas. Private Collection

6

7

8

9

10

7 Kobayashi Kokei, *Poppies*, c 1920, hanging scroll. National Museum of Art, Tokyo

8 Anonymous Japanese Artist, *Chrysanthemums*, early 19c, hanging scroll. Chester Beatty Collection, Dublin

9 Jean-Baptiste Monnoyer, *Flowerpiece with Monkey and Parrot*, late 17c, oil on canvas. Alan Jacobs Gallery, London

10 Gustav Klimt, *Roses under the Trees*, c 1905, oil on canvas. Musée d'Orsay, Paris

BELIEF

In almost every pre-modern society art and religious belief were closely linked and totemic properties were ascribed to innumerable natural and man-made objects, whether rocks and trees or carved and decorated artefacts. But such was the destructiveness of invaders and zeal of the missionaries who followed them that few such works have survived with either their meanings or their substance intact, and often we have no means of knowing what in fact they represented. Furthermore, even when written sources survive, they are often expressed in such occult terms that comprehension is either extremely difficult or impossible – the essential mysteries of native American, Polynesian, Egyptian, Greek and Roman art are good examples of this; we have the totemic objects but we lack the sources which tell us what they really signified.

We also need to remember that contact between different societies and conquest often meant that deities and belief-systems were taken over and adapted by outsiders and given quite new meanings. The Greek and Roman theogonies, for instance, were attempts to systematize various cults which had emerged throughout the ancient Middle East and Mediterranean world. Later, during the Renaissance, these gods and goddesses were depicted, if not as Christian symbols, at least as symbols which could be accommodated to Christian belief. Therefore at various times the figures of Eve and Venus, Adam and Apollo, formally at least, were essentially interchangeable, while Mars and Venus could also be depicted in contemporary guise.

On the other hand not all theologies had a tradition of religious art; the Jews for example, were forbidden to represent their holy books in figurative terms at all. It was Christian artists who increasingly turned to the Jewish Old Testament as a fertile source of narrative and dramatic subjects for art; the depiction of heaven and hell, the drama of the fall, the vicissitudes of the Jews, and the lives of their heroes and prophets became linked to parallel narratives from the New Testament and the life of Christ.

Often the theological meaning of the scene was obscured by the painter's delight in showing costume, landscape or even nudes, and sometimes the religious event was pushed into the background. The depiction of prophets and saints obviously varied according to changing belief-systems – Christ, for example, could be painted as an heroic and perfect Greek god or as the wounded Rabbinical personification of suffering humanity itself, with the events of his life, crucifixion, descent into hell and resurrection becoming at times almost the only recognized subject for artists, thus becoming the expressive stimulus for all other emotions – love, passion, guilt, despair, forgiveness and hope. Painting also gives us a clear account of the relationship between the theology of the elect and the practices of ordinary believers – whether in the intimacy of a Calvinist home or among the dozing congregation in an eighteenth-century church.

Hinduism, which, like Buddhism and Confucianism, emerged in the fifth century BC, stimulated the creation of a vast and complex art, with emphasis on the legends of various deities and semi-deities such as Krishna, Shiva and Parvati. Buddhism spread from southern India to Sri Lanka, Nepal, Burma, China (the first printed book in the world was a ninth-century Chinese Buddhist text) and Japan, till it finally reached Europe in the nineteenth century, where Buddha became a symbol, like Christ, of divine enlightenment. Traditionally, Buddhist artists tended to concentrate on the events of the life of the Buddha, his birth into a wealthy family, his acts of charity, his fasts and meditations and his death, and the tradition was extended with the Bodhisattvas,

Odilon Redon, *The Buddha,* c 1905, pastel on card. Musée d'Orsay, Paris

who personified the Buddha's enlightenment and who themselves helped souls to paradise. Islam (which means submission and obedience), like Judaism, tended to proscribe figurative art; certain scenes of the life of the Prophet Muhammad, such as his ascent into heaven, were sometimes illustrated, though characteristic scenes of Islamic pilgrimage and worship are more common.

CULTS & MYSTERIES

1 Anonymous Bolivian Artist, *Diablada Dance Mask*, 20c, painted wood and light bulbs. Horniman Museum, London

2 Anonymous Aztec Artist, *The God Quetzalcoatl* or *Tonatiuh*, c 1500, Turquoise mosaic gummed onto wood with pearl shell eyes. British Museum, London

3 Anonymous Roman Artist, *Hall of Mysteries* in Pompeii, 79 AD, fresco. Museo e Gallerie Nationali di Capodimonte, Naples

4 Anonymous Kwakiut Artist, *Revelation Mask*, 1850–60, pigment on wood. British Museum, London

5 Anonymous Rhodesian Artist, Necklace showing *Artemis* (detail), c 650 BC, gold. British Museum, London

1

2

3

4

5

6

7

8

9

6 Anonymous Egyptian Artist, *Osiris*, pectoral ornament, 18th Dynasty (c 1400 BC), Egyptian National Museum, Cairo

7 Anonymous Tahitian Sculptor, *The God A'a* from Rurutu, 19c, wood. British Museum, London

8 Anonymous Egyptian Artist, *The dead Ani, led by Horus, is brought into the presence of Osiris with the Goddesses Isis and Nephthys behind him*, 19th Dynasty (c 1250 BC), painting on papyrus. British Museum, London

9 Anonymous Native American Artist, *Tolina Divinity*, gold, 500–1500 AD. Gold Museum, Bogota

GREEK & ROMAN

1 Gianbattista Tiepolo, *Chronos Entrusting Cupid to Venus*, c 1768, oil on canvas. Private Collection

2 Raphael, *Parnassus*, 1510, fresco. Vatican, Rome

1

2

3 Odilon Redon, *The Cyclops*, c 1898–1910, oil on card. Kröller-Müller Museum, Otterlo

3

4 Nicolas Poussin, *The Feeding of Jupiter*, c 1640, oil on canvas. National Gallery of Art, Washington DC

5 Anonymous English Artist, *Jupiter, Mars and Venus, Vulcan, Cupid and the Three Graces*, c 1450, illuminated manuscript. Bodleian Library, Oxford

6 Anonymous Greek Sculptor, *Poseidon* or *Zeus* (detail), 460–450 BC, bronze. National Museum, Athens

4

5

6

7

7 Velazquez, *Triumph of Bacchus*, 1628–9, oil on canvas. Prado, Madrid

8 Sandro Botticelli, *Mars and Venus*, c 1483, tempera on panel. National Gallery, London

9 Sandro Botticelli, *The Birth of Venus*, c 1483, tempera on panel. Uffizi, Florence

8

9

10 Evelyn de Morgan, *Hero Awaiting the Return of Leander*, 1885, gouache on cardboard. Roy Miles Fine Paintings, London

11 Anatonio Pollaiuolo, *Apollo and Daphne*, c 1475, tempera on panel. National Gallery, London

12 Piero di Cosimo, *A Mythological Subject – Nymph and Faun*, c 1500, tempera on panel. National Gallery, London

10

11

12

13

14

15

13 Anonymous Roman Artist, *Bacchic Scenes with Sea Nymphs and a Marine God*, found in Mildenhall, Suffolk, 4c AD, silver. British Museum, London

14 Anonymous Greek Artist, *Odysseus and his Companions Prepare to Blind Cyclops*, c 425 BC, red figure vase painting. British Museum, London

15 Gustave Moreau, *Orpheus at the Tomb of Eurydice*, c 1891, oil on canvas. Musée Gustave Moreau, Paris

THE OLD TESTAMENT

1 William Blake, *Glad Day* or *The Dance of Albion*, c 1794, watercolour. British Museum, London

2 Anonymous French Artist, *The Creation, God Introducing Adam and Eve,* from the Moutier-Grandval Bible, 834–843, watercolour. Bibliothèque Nationale, Paris

3 Michelangelo, *The Expulsion of Adam and Eve from Paradise*, 1509–10, fresco. Sistine Chapel, Vatican, Rome

4 Anonymous French Artist, *The Story of Adam and Eve*, 9c, illuminated manuscript. British Library, London

5 Anonymous German Artist, *Noah's Ark*, from the Nuremberg Bible, 1483, woodblock. British Library, London

1

2

3

4

5

6

7

6 Rembrandt, *Moses with the Tablets of the Law*, c 1659, oil on canvas. Gemäldegalerie, Berlin

7 Anonymous French Artist, *Tree of Jesse*, from the Psalter of Ingeburg, c 1210, watercolour. Musée Condé, Chantilly

8 Nicolas Poussin, *Adoration of the Golden Calf*, 1635–7, oil on canvas. National Gallery, London

8

9

9 Albrecht Dürer, *Lot and his Daughters*, c 1498, oil on panel. Kress Collection, Washington DC

10

10 Jacopo Pontormo, *Joseph in Egypt*, 1515–16, oil on panel. National Gallery, London

11 Jean Fouquet, *The Fall of Jericho*, c 1475, watercolour. Bibliothèque Nationale, Paris

11

12 T. Flatman, *David with Head of Goliath*, 1667. watercolour miniature. Victoria and Albert Museum, London

13 Anonymous English Artist, *King David Playing his Harp*, c 1060, watercolour. British Library, London

14 Peter Paul Rubens, *Samson and Delilah*, 1610–13, oil on canvas. National Gallery, London

12

13

14

15

16

17

18

15 Workshop of Apollonio di Giovanni, *Procession of the Queen of Sheba*, 1450s, tempera on panel. Private Collection

16 Anonymous French Artist, *The Jews in the Wilderness*, 15c, watercolour. Bibliothèque Nationale, Paris

17 Giorgione, *Judith with the Head of the Tyrant Holofernes*, c 1505, oil on panel. Hermitage, St Petersburg

18 Rembrandt, *Jacob Blessing the Children of Joseph*, 1656, oil on canvas. Gemäldegalerie, Kassel

THE NEW TESTAMENT

1 Master of the Boucicault Hours, *The Visitation*, 1396–1421, watercolour and gold. Musée Jacquemart-André, Paris

2 Albrecht Dürer, *Adoration of the Kings,* 1504, oil on panel. Uffizi, Florence

3 Piero della Francesca, *The Baptism of Christ*, 1448–50, tempera on panel. National Gallery, London

4 Anonymous Italian Artist, *Christ Healing the Man of the Unclean Spirit*, 10c, ivory relief. Hessisches Landemuseum, Darmstadt

5 Daccio, *Christ Curing a Blind Man*, c 1310, tempera on panel. National Gallery, London

2

1

3

4

5

6

6 El Greco, *Christ Driving the Traders from the Temple*, c 1600, oil on canvas. National Gallery, London

7 Anonymous Flemish Artist, *The Prodigal Son*, c 1550, oil on panel. Private Collection

7

8 Ferdinand Hodler, *The Good Samaritan*, 1886, oil on canvas. Private Collection

8

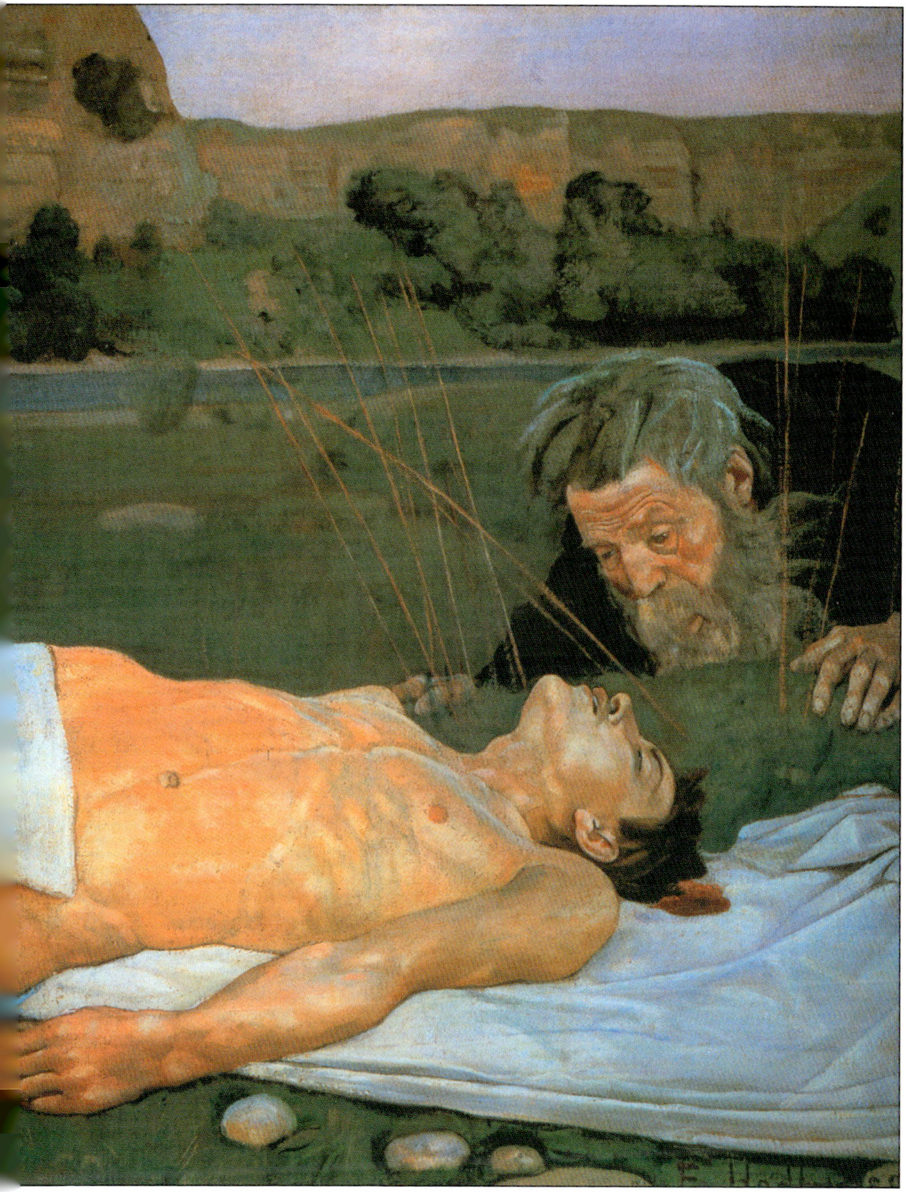

9 Anonymous French Artist, *The Last Supper* and *Christ Washing the Feet of his Disciples*, from the Psalter of Ingeburg, c 1210, watercolour. Musée Condé, Chantilly

10 Anonymous English Artist, *Christ Washing the Feet of his Disciples*, c 1480, miniature on vellum. British Library, London

11 Anthony van Dyck, *The Crowning of Christ with Thorns*, c 1620, oil on canvas. Prado, Madrid

12 Matthias Grünewald, *Christ Carrying the Cross*, c 1515, oil on panel. Staatliche Kunsthalle, Karlsruhe

13 Georges de La Tour, *St Peter's Denial of Christ*, 1650, oil on canvas. Musée des Beaux Arts, Nantes

9

10

11

12

13

14

14 Matthias Grünewald, *The Crucifixion*, c 1515, oil on panel. Staatliche Munsthalle, Karlsruhe

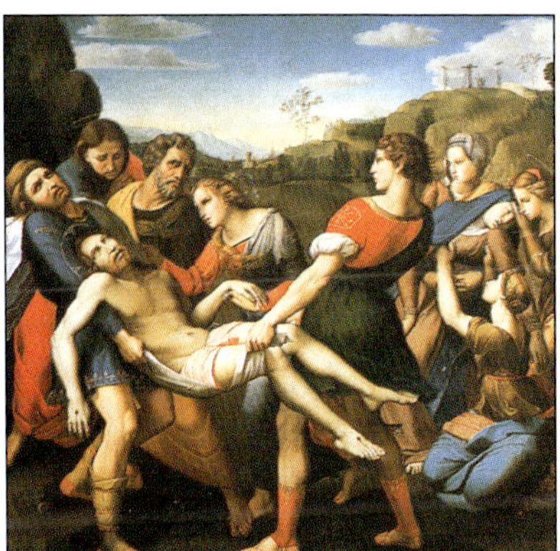

15

15 Giovanni Battista Salvi, *The Entombment*, c 1580, oil on canvas. Johnny van Haeften Gallery, London

16

16 Giovanni Bellini, *Christ's Descent into Limbo*, c 1470, tempera on panel. City Art Gallery, Bristol

17 Fra Angelico, *Noli mi Tangere*, 1441–5, fresco. Museo di San Marco, Florence

18 Matthias Grünewald, *The Resurrection*, 1512–16, oil on panel. Unterlinden Museum, Colmar

19 Raphael, *The Transfiguration*, 1517–20, oil on canvas. Vatican, Rome

20 Giovanni Bellini, *Christ Blessing*, c 1460, tempera on panel. Louvre, Paris

17

18

19

20

21

22

23

25

24

21 Anonymous English Artist, *Christ in Majesty* from the Stavelot Bible, 1093–7, watercolour. British Library, London

22 Leonardo da Vinci, *St John the Baptist*, 1513–16, oil/tempera on panel. Louvre, Paris

23 Pieter Bruegel the Younger, *St John the Baptist Preaching in the Wilderness*, (after Pieter Bruegel the Elder), c 1600, oil on canvas. Private Collection

24 Puvis de Chavannes, *The Execution of St John the Baptist*, 1869, oil on canvas. City Museum and Art Gallery, Birmingham

25 Titian, *Salome with the Head of St John the Baptist*, 1560–70, oil on canvas. Private Collection

HELL

1 Eugène Delacroix, *Dante and Virgil in the Underworld*, 1882, oil on canvas. Louvre, Paris

2 Rogier van der Weyden, *The Last Judgement* – detail of *The Resurrection of the Dead*, 1450s, oil on panel. Hôtel Dieu, Beaune

3 Rogier van der Weyden, *The Last Judgement* – detail of *Hell*, 1450s, oil on panel. Hôtel Dieu, Beaune

1

2

3

4

5

4 William Blake, *Dante and Virgil Entering Hell*, 1824–7, watercolour. Tate Gallery, London

5 Anonymous English Artist, *The Jaws of Hell Fastened by an Angel*, 1140–60, watercolour. British Library, London

6 Hieronymus Bosch, *Garden of Earthly Delights, Hell*, c 1500, oil on panel. Prado, Madrid

6

PARADISE

1 Master of Oberrheinischer, *The Garden of Paradise*, c 1410, tempera on panel. Städelsches Kunstinstitut, Frankfurt

2 Peter Paul Rubens (figures) and Jan Bruegel the Elder (landscape), *Adam and Eve in Paradise,* c 1620, oil on panel. Mauritshuis, The Hague

1

2

3

3 Edward Hicks, *The Peaceable Kingdom – William Penn's Treaty with the Indians*, c 1836, oil on panel. Philadelphia Museum of Art

4 Roelandt Savery, *Garden of Eden, Adam and Eve and All Creation*, 1620, oil on panel. Faringdon Collection Trust, Oxfordshire

4

SAINTS

1 Ludovico Carracci, *The Throwing of the Body of St Stephen into the Town Sewer*, c 1600, oil on canvas. Private Collection

2 Memling, *St Veronica,* c 1485, oil on panel. Kress Collection, National Gallery of Art, Washington DC

3 Leonardo da Vinci, *St Jerome*, c 1480, tempera/oil on panel. Vatican, Rome

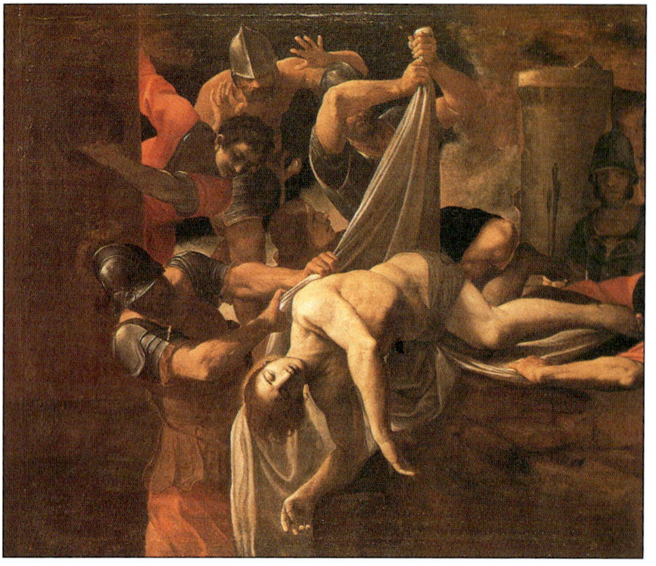

1

2

3

4

4 Adam Elsheimer, *The Stoning of St Stephen*, 1602–5, oil on canvas. National Gallery of Scotland, Edinburgh

5 Georges de La Tour, *St Joseph and the Angel*, c 1650, oil on canvas. Musée des Beaux Arts, Nantes

6 Antonio and Piero del Pollaiuolo, *Martydom of St Sebastian*, c 1476, tempera on panel. National Gallery, London

5

6

WORSHIP

1 John Collett, *George Whitfield Preaching at Moorfields*, c 1760, oil on canvas. Private Collection

2 Jean-François Millet, *The Angelus*, 1859, oil on canvas. Louvre, Paris

1

2

3

4

3 Paul Gauguin, *Vision after the Sermon,* 1888, oil on canvas. National Gallery of Scotland, Edinburgh

4 Jean Bellegambe, *The Mystical Bath – Anabaptism,* c 1530, tempera on panel. Musée des Beaux Arts, Lille

5 Lucas Cranach, *Martin Luther's Sermon,* c 1530, oil on panel. St Marie Church, Wittenberg

6 John Collett, *The Dull Sermon,* c 1760, oil on canvas. Private Collection

5

6

7

8

7 Juan de Valdes Leal, *A Jesuit Conversion,* c 1670, oil on canvas. City Art Gallery, York

8 Aert Claesz, *The Sermon,* 1510, tempera on panel. Rijksmuseum, Amsterdam

9 Pieter Neeffs the Elder, *Interior of a Dutch Church,* c 1640, oil on canvas. Johnny van Haeften Gallery, London

9

BUDDHISM

1 Anonymous Burmese Artist, *Buddhist Cosmology, Heaven*, 19c, watercolour manuscript. British Library, London

2 Anonymous Indian Sculptor, *The Death of the Buddha,* 9–10c, stone. British Museum, London

3 Anonymous Nepalese Artist, *Buddha Giving Alms,* c 1715, hanging scroll. Private Collection

4 Anonymous Japanese Artist, *Death of the Buddha (Pari-Nirvana),* 17c, handscroll. British Library, London

1

2

3

4

5

6

7

5 Anonymous Artist, *The Bodhisattva Fugen,* 12c, ink, gold and silver on silk. Freer Gallery, Smithsonian Institution, Washington DC

6 Anonymous Artist, *The Goddess Tripurasundari, the Beautiful, the Goddess of the Three Realms,* 19c, watercolour. Gulbenkian Museum of Oriental Art, Durham

7 Anonymous Chinese Artist from Tun-Huang, *The Bodhisattva Avalokitesvara Leading Souls to Paradise,* 10c, hanging scroll. British Museum, London

HINDUISM

1 Ustad Sahibdin, *Krishna Supporting Mount Govardhana*, c 1690, watercolour. British Library, London

2 Anonymous Rajasthan Artist, *Krishna as Lord of the Universe*, late 19c, watercolour. Victor Lowndes Collection, London

1

2

3

4

5

6

3 Anonymous Indian Artist, *The Holy Family of Shiva and Parvati on Mount Kailas,* c 1800, watercolour. Victoria and Albert Museum, London

4 Anonymous Syrian Artist, *The Indian Sun God,* 11c, stone. British Museum, London

5 Anonymous Rajasthan Artist, *Ramasita, Oakshman and Hamuman holding Rama's Right Foot,* c 1700, watercolour. Victoria and Albert Museum, London

6 Anonymous Garhwal Artist, *Krishna with the Cow Girl's Clothes,* c 1790, watercolour. Victoria and Albert Museum, London

ISLAM

1 Anonymous Persian Artist, *Ascent of the Prophet Muhammad Guided by the Angel Gabriel on Burag his Mule,* 1539–43, watercolour and gold on vellum. British Library, London

2 Rudolph Ernst, *The Lesson in the Mosque,* 1902, oil on canvas. Private Collection

3 Anonymous Persian Artist, *Pilgrims Going to Mecca,* 16c, watercolour. British Library, London

4 Anonymous Syrian Artist, *The Meeting of Al-Hariria, Abou Zayd Preaching in the Mosque at Samarkand,* 1300, watercolour. British Library, London

1

2

3

4

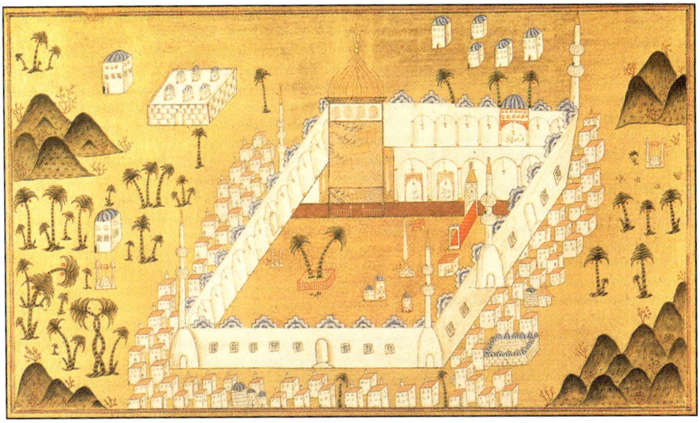
5

6

5 Anonymous Artist, *The Great Mosque at Medina,* c 1600, watercolour. Chester Beatty Collection, Dublin

6 David Roberts, *Interior of the Mosque at Metwalys,* c 1840, lithograph. Private Collection

CONFLICT

Probably no other subject in art has excited such varied responses as war. In general though, the greatest artists, like Goya and Picasso, have chosen to depict not its allegedly heroic aspect but rather its horrors. Bruegel's *Triumph of Death*, for example, is not simply a religious allegory but a description of the nightmare of a seemingly endless age of war, while *The Peaceful Kingdom*, by the Quaker and pacifist Hicks, preaches love and amity between people of different races. Even David, who had earlier been a prominent supporter of the French Revolution, chose as the subject of one of his greatest paintings the intervention of *The Sabines* – women in a battle between their fathers and brothers and the men who had first raped and then married them.

In Roman myth, war was represented by Mars, and since he is often seduced by Venus (love) the message is clear. The message of Christ (if not the actions of Christians) is also one of peace, and the same is true of Buddha, Confucius and other sages and prophets, though every religion adopted military saints like St George. In painting, what records we have of the attitudes of the past are necessarily conditioned by patterns of patronage, and insofar as history is the story of victors who have wished to commemorate their deeds and the submission of their opponents, the art which survives is in general either descriptive or celebratory. For historians, representations of war tell us much that we could never otherwise know, particularly about weaponry and fighting costumes. Battle scenes, however, are notoriously unreliable, often having been painted long after by artists who had never seen the events they heroized. For example, Altdorfer's magnificent image of war is a vivid record of an early sixteenth-century battle, and a symbol of Christian triumph over the Turks, but it tells us nothing about the actual victory of Alexander the Great over Darius the Persian in 333 BC, and to get a better notion of how the battle was actually fought we need to go to the reliefs of soldiers which decorated (and guarded) the palaces of the Persian and Assyrian kings and glorified the act of battle. European Renaissance princes, mimicking the exploits of the legendary heroes of the past liked to be portrayed in equestrian poses with the symbolic armour, plumes and eagles of antiquity.

During the eighteenth century, the mounting slaughter occasioned by new weaponry and the patterns of European warfare and colonialization resulted in attempts to make heroic the grim realities of the age. Artists like Copley and West depicted their contemporary heroes dying in classical poses, disguising the sordid nationalistic motives which occasioned their deaths.

The French Revolution had a profound impact on art. On one hand there are heroic symbols like David's icon of *The Murdered Marat in his Bath*, posed like the sacrificed Christ, the victim of misunderstanding and deceit; on the other hand there is Goya's profound indictment of the cold terror of the French Revolutionary army's savage murder of hostages after a popular revolt against French tyranny. Popular feelings in the early days are well caught by Rude's clay head of a young revolutionary leading the *sans culottes* to the barricades, the same figure in fact who inspired Delacroix's hymn to revolutionary activity, *Liberty Leading the People at the Barricades.* Likewise Manet later condemned the duplicity of the French government in the legalized murder of their puppet in *The Execution of the Emperor Maximilian.*

Modern artists, however, have tended to shrink from the horrors of total war; Kandinsky, for example, reduces the subject to folk memory of Cossack soldiers, horses and half-evoked images. In fact it was Japanese

Anonymous Hawaiin Sculptor, *War God, "Ku"*, 19c, painted wood. British Museum, London

artists like Toshiyoshi who first attempted to represent the modern technology of mass slaughter, though Lichtenstein's *Whaam!* can be read in several ways as an indictment of the comic book educated, fruit-machine playing, murderous civilization which napalmed Vietnam, or merely as a formal exercise of a mindless artist who fails to grasp the implications of such barbaric symbol systems.

WAR & PEACE

1 Lorenzo Costa, *The Garden of the Peaceful Arts – Allegory of the Court of Isabella d'Este*, c 1530, oil on panel. Louvre, Paris

2 Jacques-Louis David, *The Sabines*, 1794–9, oil on canvas. Louvre, Paris

1

2

1

2

3

HEROES

1 François Clouet, *Portrait of Francis I*, c 1545, oil on panel. Uffizi Gallery, Florence

2 Titian, *Portrait of Charles V at the Battle of Muhlberc*, 1548, oil on canvas. Prado, Madrid

3 Benjamin West, *Death of Nelson*, 1808, oil on canvas. National Maritime Museum, London

4 Charles Wilson Peale, *George Washington at Princeton*, c 1783, oil on canvas. Pennsylvania Academy of Fine Arts, Philadelphia

4

5

6

7

5 John Singleton Copley, *The Death of Major Pierson*, 1783, oil on canvas. Tate Gallery, London

6 Jacques-Louis David, *Leonidas at Thermopylae*, 1800–14, oil on canvas. Louvre, Paris

7 Benjamin West, *Death of Wolfe at the Capture of Quebec*, 1771, oil on canvas. National Gallery of Canada, Ottowa

TROOPS

1 Anonymous Greek Artist, *Two Amazons Fighting with a Greek*, 4c BC, pigment on marble. Museo Archaelogico, Florence

2 Anonymous Persian Sculptor, *Archers*, from the Palace of Artaxerxes II, Susa, 5c BC, enamel on bricks. Louvre, Paris

3 Anonymous Benin Sculptor, *The Oba Flanked by Footsoldiers*, 16c, bronze. British Museum, London

4 Anonymous Assyrian Sculptor, *Assyrian Archers Shooting from behind a Standing Shield*, 745–727 BC, stone relief. British Museum, London

1

2

3

4

5

5 Anonymous Benin Sculptor, *Portuguese Soldier Holding a Matchlock*, 16c, bronze. British Museum, London

EARLY WARFARE

1 Anonymous Mughal Artist, *Akbar Crossing the Ganges*, c 1600, watercolour. Victoria and Albert Museum, London

1

2

3

4

5

2 Anonymous French Artist, *The Expedition of the French and the Genoese to North Africa*, late 15c, illuminated manuscript. British Library, London

3 Jean de Wavrin, *The Battle of Aljubarrota in Spain*, mid 15c, illuminated manuscript. British Library, London

4 Anonymous Mughal Artist, *Takbar's Forces Besieging Ranthanbhor Fort in 1568*, 1600, illuminated manuscript. Victoria and Albert Museum, London

5 Anonymous Provincial Mughal Artist, *Battle between Persia and Turan*, mid 17c, illuminated manuscript. Victoria and Albert Museum, London

6 Albrecht Altdorfer, *Battle of Alexander*, (333 BC), 1529, oil on panel. Alte Pinakothek, Munich

7 Alexander Marshall, *The Siege of Magdeburg*, 16c, oil on canvas. Private Collection

6

7

8

8 Anonymous French Artist, *Assault on a Strong Town in Africa*, late 15c, watercolour. British Library, London

9 Quinte Curse, *Soldiers Armed with Handcannon Besieging a Castle*, c 1468, watercolour. British Library, London

10 Anonymous French Artist, *Knights on Horseback*, 15c, watercolour. Bibliothèque Nationale, Paris

9

10

REVOLUTION

1 Louis van Blarenberghe, *Surrender of Yorktown*, c 1785, oil on canvas. Château, Versailles

2 Goya, *The Second of May 1808, Mameluke Soldiers Attacking the People during the Spanish Revolt*, 1814, oil on canvas. Prado, Madrid

3 Eugène Delacroix, *Liberty Leading the People at the Barricades*, 1830, oil on canvas. Louvre, Paris

4 Goya, *The Third of May 1808, Execution of the Revolutionaries*, 1814, oil on canvas. Prado, Madrid

1

2

3

4

5

5 Anonymous Indian Artist, *An Incident during the Indian Mutiny*, 1857, watercolour. National Army Museum, London

6 Edouard Manet, *The Execution of the Emperor Maximilian*, 1867, oil on canvas. Städtische Kunsthalle, Mannheim

6

THE FRENCH REVOLUTION

1 Jules-Claude Ziegler, *The Republic*, 1848, oil on canvas. Musée des Beaux Arts, Lille

2 Johann Zoffany, *The 10th August 1782 – Plunder of the King's Wine Cellar*, c 1783, oil on canvas. Brod Gallery, London

3 Antoine-Jean Gros, *Napoleon Visiting the Plague Victims at Jaffa*, 1804, oil on canvas. Louvre, Paris

4 Antoine-Jean Gros, *The Young Napoleon on the Bridge of Arcole*, 1796, oil on canvas. Louvre, Paris

5 Anonymous French Artist, *Charlotte Corday*, c 1792, oil on canvas. Château, Versailles

1

2

3

4

5

6

7

8

9

6 Jacques-Louis David, *The Murdered Marat in his Bath*, 1793, oil on canvas. Musée Royaux des Beaux Arts, Brussels

7 François Rude, *Departure of the Volunteers, in 1792, "The Marseillaise"*, 1833–6, clay model for sculptures on the Arc de Triomphe, Paris. Louvre, Paris

8 George Morland, *The Pressgang*, 1790, oil on canvas. Royal Holloway College, London

9 Hubert Robert, *The Demolition of the Bastille*, 1789, oil on canvas. Musée Carnavalet, Paris

10 Antoine-Jean Gros, *Napoleon at the Battle of Eylau*, 1808, oil on canvas. Louvre, Paris

10

WAR AT SEA

1 Philippe de Loutherbourg, *The Cutting out of the French Corvette "La Chevrette"*, 1801, oil on canvas. City Art Gallery, Bristol

2 Anonymous Artist, *The Mêlée on board the Chesapeake in 1813*, c 1815, watercolour. Private Collection

1

2

3

3 Pedro Barreto de Resende, *The English Repelling Portuguese Ships at Swally Hole in 1630*, 1646, watercolour. British Library, London

4 Anonymous English Artist, *The Armada*, c 1510, oil on panel. Society of Apothecaries, London

4

MODERN WAR

1 Toshiyoshi, *Terrible War of General Sakamoto*, 1894, woodcut print. Private Collection

2 Umberto Boccioni, *A Fight in the Arcade*, 1910, oil on canvas. Jesi Collection, Milan

1

2

3 Henri Rousseau, *War – La Chevauchée de la Discorde*, 1894, oil on canvas. Louvre, Paris

3

4 Henry Moore, *Tube Shelter*, 1941, Tate Gallery, London

5 Roy Lichtenstein, *Whaam!*, 1963, diptych, oil on canvas. Tate Gallery, London

4

5

6

6 Wassily Kandinsky, *Battle – the Cossacks*, 1910, oil on canvas. Tate Gallery, London

7 Paul Nash, *We are Making a New World*, 1918, oil on canvas. Imperial War Museum, London

7

ANIMALS

The terrors of the wild and the difficulties of travel made animals like griffons, unicorns, centaurs and dragons seem quite real to the imaginations of early artists. Such mythical animals also symbolized quite diverse characteristics like lust (the centaur), fidelity and purity (the unicorn) and evil (the dragon), though in China and Japan the dragon was a symbol of wisdom. For later artists some of those associations remained but mythical animals like Redon's *Chimera* also came to represent more general psychological states of mind.

Particular animals were often associated with various cults and divinities. The ancient Egyptians, for example, tamed and venerated cats, while the ram, in ancient Mesopotamia, was both a sacrificial victim and a symbol of rebirth – meanings which passed into Judaism and Christianity and can be seen in pictures like *The Sacrifice of Isaac by Abraham* and Holman Hunt's miserable *Scapegoat*. We do not know why early cave-dwellers painted bison, deer and other animals on the walls of their caves but it seems likely that the pictures were venerated in various ways and related to the return of the herds of wild animals with the seasons. The cultic massacre of certain animals like the bull survives to remind us of these ancient rituals.

Quite early on, particular deities were associated with specific animals – Dionysus-Bacchus with the leopard, the Buddha with the elephant, Christ with the lamb, the fish and the donkey and so on. Saints too had their animals; the humility of St Francis was associated with birds, St Jerome was protected by his symbolic lion (which in Europe was a symbol of Africa), while in Chinese art the lion became the ubiquitous Buddhist guardian spirit of the home.

Images of alligators fighting pythons, tigers attacking elephants and lions attacking people reveal quite different motives – fear and the attempt to master the terrors of the wild. Stubbs' many paintings of horses being ripped apart by lions reveal an obsession occasioned both by classical treatments of the subject and by his witnessing of such an event while travelling in north Africa.

In many places certain wild animals were sanctified and thus (in the imagination at least) tamed, while artists like Piero di Cosimo in *The Forest Fire* and Marc in his *Horse in a Landscape* represented animals as both victims and symbols of human cruelty and suffering.

The shift of people from the countryside to towns and early cities went hand in hand with the taming of many hitherto wild animals. Horses and elephants were trained for war and sport, and in particular for hunting, a subject which attracted artists in ancient Greece and Mughal India as well as medieval Europe. Since people in general prefer the taste of venison to horsemeat, horses were ennobled and deer were massacred to satisfy the paunches of kings, though the slaughter of animals for sport became, for artists like Goya and Picasso, symbols of the horrors of war itself.

Only when humans had begun to occupy the countryside in relative safety did artists begin to depict shy and evasive wild animals such as rabbits, hares and squirrels. Indian artists like Mansur and Japanese artists like Taito and Chinzan were particularly adept at capturing such fugitive subjects. European artists meanwhile often accompanied overseas expeditions and the fauna they captured, depicted and brought back soon filled the farmyards, aviaries and pictures of European collectors. Exotic birds, in particular, became both the target of collectors and the subject for painters.

Other animals, like dogs, when tamed and trained, came to symbolize bravery and fidelity. Ownership of a

Hieronymus Bosch, *The Garden of Earthly Delights,* left panel from *The Garden of Eden,* 1485, oil on panel. Prado, Madrid

well-bred dog, prize bulls and sheep and an Arab horse became, for the eighteenth-century gentleman, emblems of his own good breeding, potency and wealth, and artists like Stubbs (whose obsession extended to the dissection of slowly rotting corpses in freezing barns) and Géricault (who died after falling off a horse) transformed horse-painting into a distinct genre.

MYTHIC ANIMALS

1 Paolo Uccello, *St George Slaying the Dragon*, c 1456, tempera on panel. National Gallery, London

2 Sadahide, *A Dragon and Two Tigers*, 1858, woodblock print. Victoria and Albert Museum, London

3 Anonymous Persian Sculptor, *Two Griffons*, 6c BC, enamel bricks. Louvre, Paris

1

2

3

4

6

5

7

4 Anonymous French Artist, *The Virgin with the Unicorn*, c 1500, tapestry. Musée de Cluny, Paris

5 George Frederick Watts, *The Minotaur*, 1885, oil on canvas. Tate Gallery, London

6 Anonymous Artist, *Daniel's Vision of the Four Beasts and God Enthroned*, 1109, watercolour from Mozarabic Bible – Silos Apocalypse. British Library, London

7 Gustave Moreau, *Dead Poet Borne by a Centaur*, c 1890, oil on canvas. Musée Gustave Moreau, Paris

SYMBOLIC

1 Anonymous Sumerian Artist, *Ram* – symbol of fertility, c 2500 BC, shell, gold, silver, lapis lazuli and bitumen on wood. British Museum, London

2 Anonymous Late Magdalenian Artist, *Bison*, c 15,000 BC?, cave painting. Altamira, Spain

3 William Holman Hunt, *The Scapegoat*, 1854, oil on canvas. Lady Lever Art Gallery, Port Sunlight, Merseyside

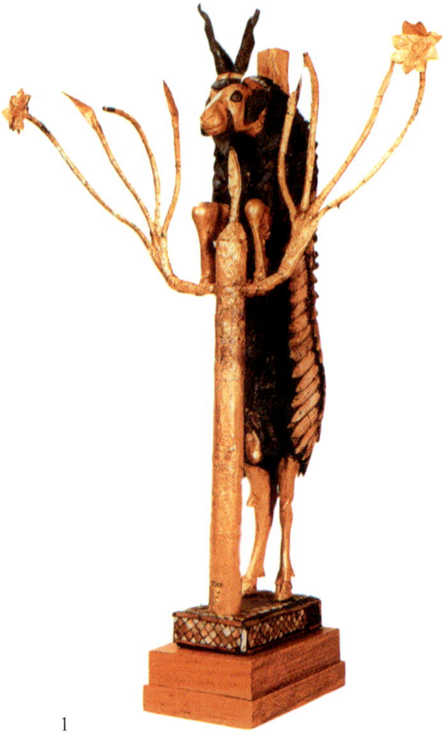

1

3

2

4 Anonymous Egyptian Jeweller, *Scarab*, 18th Dynasty (c 1340 BC), from Tutankhamen's Tomb. Egyptian National Museum, Cairo

5 Anonymous Greek Artist, *Dionysus Riding a Leopard*, 4c BC, mosaic. House of Masks, Delos

4

5

AQUATIC

1 Taito, *Carp*, 1848, woodblock print. Victoria and Albert Museum, London

2 Tsubaki Chinzan, *Fish*, c 1840, woodblock print. British Museum, London

3 Tsubaki Chinzan, *Crab*, c 1840, watercolour, from *Album of Birds, Flowers and Fish*. British Museum, London

4 Thomas Baines, *Thomas Baines and C. Humphrey Killing an Alligator*, 1856, oil on canvas. Royal Geographical Society, London

5 Katsushika Hokusai, *Whaling off Goto Island from Oceans of Wisdom*, 1830–3, woodblock print. Private Collection

1

2

3

4

5

1

2

4

3

5

INSECTS

1 Anonymous Japanese Artist, 19c, hanging scroll. Chester Beatty Collection, Dublin

2 Anonymous French Jeweller, *Butterfly*, mid 19c, glass paperweight. Private collection, London

3 Shibato Junzo Zeshin, *Rice and Cricket*, c 1840, watercolour. British Museum, London

4 Maedawa Bunrei, *Flowers and Insects*, 1909, watercolour. Private Collection

5 Anonymous Flemish Artist, *Insects and Flowers*, c 1500, watercolour. Victoria and Albert Museum, London

BIRDS

1 Anonymous Chinese Artist, Pair of *Geese*, 18c, bronze. Private Collection

2 Anonymous Egyptian Artist, *Marsh Scene*, 18th Dynasty (c 1400 BC), tempera on plaster. Valley of the Nobles, Thebes

3 The Chinese Emperor Chao Chi (Hui Tsung), *Birds and Flowers* (detail), c 1100, ink and colour on silk. British Library, London

4 Utanosoke Ganku, *Birds and Flowers*, c 1800, watercolour. Private Collection

1

2

3

4

5

6

7

8

5 Henry Stacey Marks, *Indian Crane, Cockatoo, Bullfinch and Thrush*, 19c, oil on canvas. Private Collection

6 Kaburagi Sejin Baikei, *Pheasants*, c 1790, ink and colour on silk. British Museum, London

7 John James Audubon, *Whooping Crane* from *Birds of America*, 1827, lithograph. British Museum, London

8 Mansur, *Himalayan Chear Pheasant*, c 1620, watercolour. Victoria and Albert Museum, London

9 William Hart, *Blue Bird of Paradise*, 19c, lithograph. British Museum, London

10 Pieter Casteels, *Grey Heron, Turkey Cock and Pheasants*, 1720, oil on canvas. Roy Miles Fine Paintings, London

11 Jan van Kessel, *Decorative Fowl and Ducklings*, 17c, oil on canvas. Johnny van Haeften Gallery, London

9

10

11

12

13

14

15

12 Jakob Bogdani, *Fruit and Birds*, early 18c, oil on canvas. Roy Miles Fine Paintings, London

13 Tobias Strannover, *Wild Fowl* (detail), early 18c, oil on canvas. Private Collection

14 John James Audubon, *Tulip Tree*, from *Birds of America,* 1827. lithograph. British Museum, London

15 John Gould and William Hart, *Pharomacrus Mocinno*, 1875, coloured engraving. Natural History Museum, London

WILD

1 Piero di Cosimo, *The Forest Fire*, c 1510, oil on panel. Ashmolean Museum, Oxford

2 Jacob Bouttats, *Garden of Eden*, c 1700, oil on canvas. Private Collection

1

2

3 Jacob Savery II, *The Animals Entering Noah's Ark*, c 1620, oil on canvas. Private Collection

3

4 Shibato Junzo Zeshin, *Monkey and Rainbow*, c 1840, watercolour. British Museum, London

5 George Stubbs, *Portrait of a Monkey*, 1774, oil on canvas. Private Collection

6 Albrecht Dürer, *The Hare*, 1502, watercolour. Albertina, Vienna

7 Anonymous Kano School Artist, *Rabbits and Grasses*, 18c, watercolour on screen. British Museum, London

4

5

6

7

8

9

10

11

12

13

8 Maria Sybille Merian, *Alligator and Python*, 1730, coloured print. Victoria and Albert Museum, London

9 Albrecht Dürer, *The Rhinoceros*, 1515, woodblock from two blocks. Private Collection

10 Théodore Géricault, *Study of a Lion*, c 1812, oil on canvas. Private Collection

11 Mansur, *A Zebra*, c 1620, watercolour. Victoria and Albert Museum, London

12 John James Audubon, *Prairie Dog* from *Quadrupeds of America*, 1842–5, lithograph. Victoria and Albert Museum, London

13 John James Audubon, *Polar Bear*, from *Quadrupeds of America*, 1842–5, lithograph. Victoria and Albert Museum, London

14 Abu'l Hasan, *Squirrels in a Plane Tree*, c 1610, watercolour. Private Collection

14

15

15 George Stubbs, *Horse Devoured by a Lion*, 1763, oil on canvas. Tate Gallery, London

16

16 Anonymous Kotah Artist, *Raja Goman Singh Shooting Lions*, 1778, watercolour. Victoria and Albert Museum, London

DOMESTIC

1 Gaston Sébus, *Stag Hunting*, c 1390, watercolour. Bibliothèque Nationale, Paris

2 Anonymous Central Indian Artist, *Shivagi on Horseback*, c 1700, water and body colour on paper. Bibliothèque Nationale, Paris

3 Franz Marc, *Horse in a Landscape*, 1910, oil on canvas. Folkwang Museum, Essen

1

2

3

4

5

4 Théodore Géricault, *Dapple-Grey Horse*, c 1817, oil on canvas. Private Collection

5 Paul Gauguin, *The White Horse*, 1898, oil on canvas. Louvre, Paris

6 Franz Marc, *Two Cats*, 1912, oil on canvas. Kunstmuseum, Basel

7 Anonymous English Artist, *Stable Animals*, mid 19c, oil on canvas. Private Collection

8 Karl Kaspar Pitz, *Dog and Hare*, c 1785, oil on canvas. Roy Miles Fine Paintings, London

9 Anonymous English Artist, *Still Life with Cat and Mouse*, c 1820, oil on panel. Private Collection

6

7

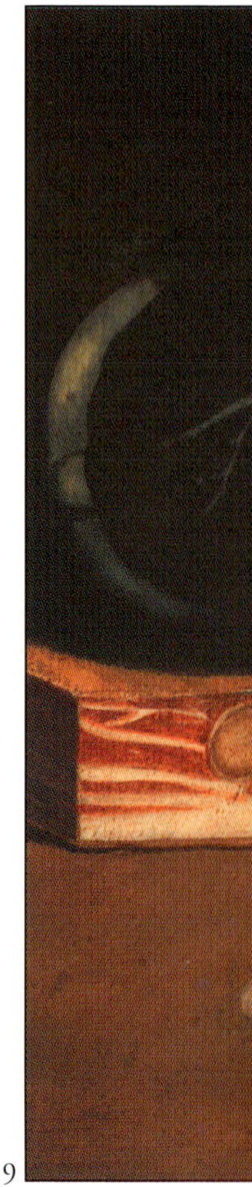

9

8

10 Horatio Henry Couldery, *Cats*, c 1860, oil on canvas. Private Collection

11 Marie-Yvonne Laur, *Little Treasures*, c 1900, oil on canvas. Private Collection

10

11

12 Jean-Louis Demarne, *La Sortie des Bestiaux*, c 1790, oil on canvas. Private Collection

13 Anonymous Mughal Artist, *A Youth with a Buck on a Lead*, early 18c, watercolour. Victoria and Albert Museum, London

14 Anonymous Chinese Sculptor, *A Bactrian Camel*, T'ang Dynasty (618–907 AD), earthenware with brown glaze. Gulbenkian Museum of Oriental Art, Durham

15 William Millner, *Feeding the Chickens*, mid 19c, oil on canvas. Private Collection

12

13

14

15

16

17

18

19

16 Jean-Baptiste Oudry, *The Farm*, 1750, oil on canvas. Louvre, Paris

17 William J. Shayer, *Cockerels*, mid 19c, oil on canvas. Private Collection

18 A. Jackson, *Chickens and Ducks in a Farmyard*, 1886, oil on canvas. Private Collection

19 Giuseppe Pellizza da Volpedo, *Deluded Hopes*, late 19c, oil on canvas. Private Collection

THE ARTIST'S LIFE

An interest in the working conditions of artists, what they looked like, how they were trained, the relation of the artist and patron, the role of the connoisseur and dealer and the nature of the art market, are all relatively recent subjects in European art, and, with the exception of Japan, rarely encountered outside Europe. Such pictures were often contemptuous, like Rowlandson's and Daumier's satirical comments on pretentious connoisseurs and critics, though occasionally, as in van Gogh's portrait of the dealer *Père Tanguy* surrounded by Japanese prints and unsold pictures by his unknown friends, they are characterized by great affection and warmth.

Portraits of the artist were, of course, often shown in Renaissance paintings – Raphael included portraits of himself, Leonardo and Bramante in *The School of Athens*, and apprentices like the young Bronzino were often posed by their masters (Bronzino is The Study in the foreground of Pontormo's *Joseph in Egypt*). But the subject of the artist at work in his studio appears largely to have been a Flemish and a Dutch invention. By the eighteenth century the artist's education came increasingly to depend upon knowledge of the old masters, which was gained through copying "old masters" and studying classical sculpture. Often such training was supervised by Academies.

Courbet's great allegory, *The Artist's Studio*, derives part of its potency by contrasting the idealized activities of academy artists with the actual world of the artist, surrounded by beggars, pick-pockets and financiers, as well as his friends like Baudelaire (sitting reading) and his supporters, though the artist himself at work is the focus of the painting.

Bazille shows *The Artist's Studio* as a meeting place of friends for debate, recreation and work, and Manet took the subject of the artist at work to stress the novel working conditions of late nineteenth-century avant garde artists as in his portrait of *Monet in his Floating Studio.*

The self-portrait as a subject in its own right also emerged during the Renaissance, when patrons, and to a lesser extent the public, began to celebrate the achievements of individual artists, and when any work by particular artists was collected, irrespective of the subject depicted. Rembrandt, however, was again exceptional. Throughout his life he painted over a hundred self-portraits, sometimes as dual portraits of himself and his wife Saskia, but, increasingly as he got older, as meditations on his own mortality and decay. Goya, greatly influenced by Rembrandt, also produced a number of ironic and revelatory self-portraits. Courbet painted himself being greeted as an equal by his patron, an image which Gauguin later mocked in his own satirical self-portrait which stresses the poverty and exclusion of the artist from the world of bourgeois respectability. Rousseau, conversely, portrayed himself in his Sunday clothes as a respectable bourgeois, with an iron bridge, the Eiffel Tower and a balloon behind him as emblems of his interest in contemporary life. Van Gogh's profound acknowledgment of his own madness and pain, as seen in his *Self-portrait with Bandaged Ear*, was however something quite new in art, and the influence of this kind of confessional self-portrait on later artists was enormous.

Ernst Ludwig Kirchner, *Self-portrait with Model*, c 1913, oil on canvas. Kunsthalle, Hamburg

THE STUDIO

1 Gerard Dou, *The Painter in his Studio*, c 1650, oil on canvas. Private Collection

2 Théodore Géricault, *Young Artist at his Easel*, c 1812, oil on canvas. Private Collection

1

2

4

3

5

6

3 Jan Vermeer, *The Painter's Studio*, c 1665–70, oil on canvas. Kunsthistorisches Museum, Vienna

4 Joseph Wright, *Academy by Lamplight*, 1765, oil on canvas. Mellon Collection, Upperville, Virginia

5 Jean-Baptiste Chardin, *A Young Draughtsman Copying an Academy Study*, c 1730, oil on canvas. Private Collection

6 Francis Wheatley, *The Royal Academy School*, c 1790, oil on canvas. Lady Lever Art Gallery, Port Sunlight, Merseyside

7 Gustave Courbet, *The Artist's Studio*, 1854–5, oil on canvas. Louvre, Paris

8 Frederic Bazille, *The Artist's Studio*, c 1869–70, oil on canvas. Musée d'Orsay, Paris

7

8

9

9 Edouard Manet, *Eva Gonzalès*, 1869–70, oil on canvas. National Gallery, London

10 Edouard Manet, *Monet in his Floating Studio*, 1874, oil on canvas. Alte Pinakothek, Munich

10

THE MARKET

1 Louis-Léopold Boilly, *Print Collectors*, c 1820, oil on canvas. Louvre, Paris

2 Honoré Daumier, *The Print Collectors*, 1850s, chalk, pen and ink. Victoria and Albert Museum, London

3 Thomas Rowlandson, *Indian Picture Dealers Humbugging the English Milord*, 1812, colour print. British Library, London

1

2

3

4

4 Vincent van Gogh, *Portrait of Père Tanguy,* the paint and picture dealer, 1887, oil on canvas. Musée Rodin, Paris

5

5 Anonymous, *Sale at Christies in the 1830s*, 1830s, ink and wash. Private Collection

SELF-PORTRAITS

1 Filippino Lippi, *Self-portrait*, c 1480, tempera on panel. Uffizi Gallery, Florence

2 Raphael, *Self-portrait*, c 1505, tempera on panel. Uffizi Gallery, Florence

3 Albrecht Dürer, *Self-portrait*, 1498, oil on panel. Prado, Madrid

4 Sophonisba Angusciola, *Self-portrait*, c 1560, oil on canvas. The Manor House, Stanton Harcourt, Oxfordshire

1

2

3

4

5

5 Peter Paul Rubens, *Self-portrait*, c 1605, oil on canvas. Private Collection

6 Rembrandt, *Self-portrait*, c 1665, oil on canvas. Iveagh Bequest, Kenwood House, London

7 Goya, *Self-portrait aged 69*, 1815, oil on canvas. Kunsthistorisches Museum, Vienna

8 Goya, *Self-portrait*, c 1817–19, oil on canvas. Prado, Madrid

6

7

8

9

10

9 Jacques-Louis David, *Self-portrait*, c 1775, oil on canvas. Louvre, Paris

10 Caspar David Friedrich, *Self-portrait*, 1802, pencil and wash. Kunsthalle, Hamburg

11 Gustave Courbet, *Bonjour Monsieur Courbet*, 1854, oil on canvas. Musée Fabre, Montpellier

11

12 Paul Gauguin, *Bonjour Monsieur Gauguin*, 1889–90, oil on canvas. Private Collection

12

13

14

13 Henri Rousseau, *Self-portrait*, c 1895, oil on canvas. Narodni Galerie, Prague

14 Vincent van Gogh, *Self-portrait with Bandaged Ear*, 1889, oil on canvas. Courtauld Institute Galleries, London

15 Umberto Boccioni, *Self-portrait*, 1908, oil on canvas. Brera Gallery, Milan

15

BIBLIOGRAPHY

GENERAL

A World of History of Art, Hugh Honour and John Fleming, Papermac, 1981

The Story of Art, E.H. Gombrich, Phaidon, 1984

History of Art, H.W. Janson, Thames & Hudson, 1986

The Story of Modern Art, Norbert Lynton, Phaidon, 1980

The Oxford Companion to Art, ed. Harold Osborne, Oxford University Press, 1970

The Penguin Dictionary of Art and Artists, Peter and Linda Murray, Penguin, 1986

Pictures as Arguments, Hans Hess, Sussex University Press, 1975

Art in Society, Ken Baynes, Lund-Humphries, 1973

ICONOGRAPHY

An Illustrated Encyclopedia of Traditional Symbols, J.C. Cooper, Thames & Hudson, 1978

Animals with Human Faces – a guide to animal symbolism, Beryl Rowland, George Allen & Unwin, 1973

Signs and Symbols in Christian Art, George Ferguson, Oxford University Press, 1966

Man and his Symbols, Carl Jung, Aldus, 1964

Allegory and the Migration of Symbols, Rudolf Wittkower, Thames & Hudson, 1977

A Dictionary of Classical Mythology, Pierre Grimal, Blackwell, 1986

A Dictionary of Chinese Symbols, Wolfram Eberhard, Thames & Hudson, 1986

A Dictionary of Egyptian Gods and Goddesses, George Hart, Routledge & Kegan Paul, 1986

The Gods and Symbols of Ancient Egypt, Manfred Linket, Thames & Hudson, 1984

The World of Islam, ed. Bernard Lewis, Thames & Hudson, 1976

The World of Buddhism, ed. Heinz Bechert and Richard Grombich, Thames & Hudson, 1984

Buddhism, Art and Faith, ed. W. Zwalf, British Museum Publications, 1985

The Art of Tantra, Philip Rawson, Thames & Hudson, 1978

AFRICAN ART

A Short History of African Art, Werner Gillon, Penguin, 1986

African Art, Frank Willet, Thames & Hudson, 1971

Egyptian Art, Cyril Aldred, Thames & Hudson, 1980

AMERICAN ART

The Art of Meso – America, Mary Ellen Miler, Thames & Hudson, 1986

CHINESE ART

Chinese Art, Mary Tregear, Thames & Hudson, 1980

Chinese Painting, Nicole Vandier-Nicolas, Lund Humphries, 1983

INDIAN ART

The Arts of India, ed. Basil Gray, Phaidon, 1981

Indian Art, Roy C. Craven, Thames & Hudson, 1976

JAPANESE ART

Japanese Art, Joan Stanley-Baker, Thames & Hudson, 1984

Art of the Edo Period, 1660–1868, ed. William Watson, Weidenfeld & Nicolson, 1981

POLYNESIAN ART

The Art of Tahiti, Terence Barrow, Thames & Hudson, 1979

EUROPEAN ART

A Shorter History of Greek Art, Martin Robinson, Cambridge University Press, 1981

A Handbook of Roman Art, Martin Hering, Phaidon, 1986

Early Medieval Art, John Beckwith, Thames & Hudson, 1969

The Rise of the Artist, Andrew Martindale, Thames & Hudson, 1972

Painting in Florence and Siena after the Black Death, Millard Meiss, Harper & Row, 1951

Early Renaissance, Michael Levey, Penguin, 1967

The Art of the Renaissance, Peter and Linda Murray, Thames & Hudson, 1963

Venetian Painting, John Steer, Thames & Hudson, 1970

The Renaissance and Mannerism outside Italy, Alistair Smart, Thames & Hudson, 1972

Dutch Painting, R.H. Fuchs, Thames & Hudson, 1978

Mannerism, John Shearman, Penguin, 1967

Mannerism, Arnold Hauser, Havard, 1986

Baroque and Rococo, Germain Bazin, Thames & Hudson, 1964

Rococo and Revolution, Michael Levey, Thames & Hudson, 1966

Romantic Art, William Vaughan, Thames & Hudson, 1978

Romanticism, Hugh Honour, Penguin, 1979

Neo-Classicism, Hugh Honour, Penguin, 1968

Watercolours, Graham Reynolds, Thames & Hudson, 1971

Emblem and Expression – Meaning in English Art of the Eighteenth Century, Ronald Paulson, Thames & Hudson, 1975

The Absolute Bourgeois, T.J. Clark, Thames & Hudson, 1973

Image of the People, T.J. Clark, Thames & Hudson, 1973

The Painting of Modern Life, T.J. Clark, 1984

Impressionism, Phoebe Pool, Thames & Hudson, 1967

Woman Impressionists, Tamar Garb, Phaidon, 1986

Symbolist Art, Edward Lucie-Smith, Thames & Hudson, 1984

The Expressionists, Worlf-Dieter Dube, Thames & Hudson, 1972

Modern Painting and the Northern Romantic Tradition, Friedrich to Rothko, Robert Rosenblum, Thames & Hudson, 1978

INDIVIDUAL ARTISTS

William Blake, Katherine Raine, Thames & Hudson, 1970

Bosch, Carl Linfert, Abrams, NY, 1982

Hieronymus Bosch, Walter S. Gibson, Thames & Hudson, 1973

The Complete Paintings of Botticelli, Gabriele Mandel, Penguin, 1985

Bruegel, Walter S. Gibson, Oxford University Press, 1977

Canaletto, J.G. Links, Phaidon, 1982

Mary Cassatt, Griselda Pollock, Jupiter, 1980

Cézanne, John Rewald, Thames & Hudson, 1986

Chardin, Philp Conisbee, Phaidon, 1986

Constable, Michael Rosenthal, Yale University Press, 1983

Corot, Madeleine Hous, Abrams, NY 1983

Dali, Dawn Ades, Thames & Hudson, 1982

David, Anita Brookner, Chatto & Windus, 1980

Degas, Daniel Catton Rich, Thames & Hudson, 1985

The Art of Albrecht Dürer, Heinrich Wolfflin, Phaidon, 1971

The Complete Paintings of the van Eycks, Giorgio T. Faggin, Penguin, 1986

Goya and the Impossible Revolution, Gwyn Williams, Allen Lane, 1976

Goya, Jose Gudiol, Abrams, NY, 1980

George Grosz, Hans Hess, Studio Vista, 1974

Hogarth, Frederick Antal, Routledge & Kegan Paul, 1962

Holbein, John Rowlands, Phaidon, 1985

Klee and Nature, Richard Vendi, Zwemmer, 1984

Gustav Klimt, Alessandra Comini, Thames & Hudson, 1975

Manet, The Metropolitan Museum of Art Exhibition Catalogue, Thames & Hudson, 1984

Michelangelo, Linda Murray, Thames & Hudson, 1980

Millet, Griselda Pollock, Oresko, 1977

Paula Modersohn-Becker, Gill Perry, Womens Press, 1979

Modigliani, Douglas Hall, Phaidon, 1979

Claude Monet, Joel Isaacson, Phaidon, 1978

Berthe Morisot, Jean Dominique Rey, Crown, NY, 1982

Edvard Munch, J.P. Hodin, Thames & Hudson, 1984

The Paintings of Samuel Palmer, Raymond Lister, Cambridge, 1985

Picasso, Timothy Hilton, Thames & Hudson, 1975

Pissarro, John Rewald, Abrams, NY, 1984

Jackson Pollock, Elizabeth Frink, Abbeville, NY, 1983

Poussin, Christopher Wright, Harlequin, 1985

Raphael, Roger Jones and Nicholas Penny, Yale, 1983

Redon, Jean Selz, Crown, 1978

Rembrandt, Gary Schwartz, Viking, 1985
Renoir, Catalogue to Arts Council of Great Britain Exhibition, Abrams, NY, 1985
Henri Rousseau, Museum of Modern Art New York Exhibition Catalogue, MOMA, 1985
The World of Henri Rousseau, Yani le Pichon, Viking, 1986
Egon Schiele, Alessandra Comini, Thames & Hudson, 1986
Turner, Graham Reynolds, Thames & Hudson, 1969
Van Gogh, Meyer Schapiro, Abrams, NY, 1982
Velazquez, Joseph-Emile Muller, Thames & Hudson, 1976
Vermeer, Arthur K. Wheelock Jr., Abrams, NY, 1983
Watteau, Donald Posner, Weidenfeld & Nicolson, 1984

THEMES IN ART

The Nude, Kenneth Clark, Penguin, 1960
The Nude in Western Art, Malcolm Cormack, Phaidon, 1976
Monuments and Maidens, Marina Warner, Picador, 1985
Flowers in Art, Paul Hutton & Lawrence Smith, British Museum, 1979
Images of Man and Death, Philippe Aries, Havard, 1985
Musical Instruments and their Symbolism in Western Art, Emanuel Winternitz, Yale University Press, 1967
Born Under Saturn, Rudolf and Margot Wittkower, Norton, 1963
The Painter Depicted, Michael Levey, Thames & Hudson, 1982

INDEX

Compiled by Hilary Bird

C

M

N